MORE PRAISE FOR **GUARDIAN OF THE REPUBLIC**

"*Guardian of the Republic* is not simply the title of this powerful book. It's what the founders demanded of each of us: to be sentinels for freedom. Allen West is such a soldier. From the battlefields of Iraq and Afghanistan to the combat of Capitol Hill and beyond, he has fought tirelessly and fearlessly for the American idea. This is a passionate clarion call to restore that idea—'the last best hope of earth,' in the words of Lincoln—before it's too late."

> —MONICA CROWLEY, PhD, host of *The Monica Crowley Show* and *New York Times* bestselling author of *What the (Bleep) Just Happened?*

"Allen West is an interesting and impressive man, and he tells a gripping and fascinating tale. Read it. You'll learn about war, politics, America . . . and life."

> —WILLIAM KRISTOL, editor, *The Weekly Standard*

"*Guardian of the Republic* is a refreshing account of one man's journey—through obstacle and opportunity and aided by faith and family—to become a warrior for the future of the American republic. Allen West's story is rooted in education, self-reliance, and a relentless sense of purpose. He strips away the pretenses of liberalism and reminds us what's at stake if we continue to make the wrong choices. Most inspiringly, he offers readers an invitation to stand strong on behalf of those values that have defined generations of Americans."

> —MICHAEL STEELE, former chairman of the Republican National Committee

GUARDIAN OF THE REPUBLIC

GUARDIAN OF THE REPUBLIC

* *

AN AMERICAN RONIN'S JOURNEY TO

FAITH, FAMILY, AND FREEDOM

ALLEN WEST

WITH MICHELE HICKFORD

CROWN
FORUM
NEW YORK

Copyright © 2014 by Allen West

All rights reserved.
Published in the United States by Crown Forum, an imprint of the
Crown Publishing Group, a division of Random House LLC, a
Penguin Random House Company, New York.

www.crownpublishing.com

CROWN FORUM with colophon is a registered trademark of
Random House LLC.

Library of Congress Cataloging-in-Publication Data is available
upon request.

ISBN 978-0-8041-3810-9
eBook ISBN 978-0-8041-3811-6

Printed in the United States of America

Book design by Lauren Dong
Jacket design by Michael Nagin
Jacket photography by Jeffrey Salter

10 9 8 7 6 5 4 3 2 1

First Edition

CONTENTS

Contents

PROLOGUE

What would I like you to take away from this book? My goal is simple: to provide insight into who I am and the journey that brought me here today.

Scores of reporters, journalists, pundits, bloggers, opponents, and strangers have done their darndest to paint a particular picture of me and typecast me to fit their narrative. In this day and age, when "news" and "reporting" have become tools to further an agenda instead of the means of presenting the facts, it's not always easy to communicate the truth.

So rather than offer a conventional autobiography, I'd like to share with you my philosophical beliefs and the reasons why I love this country and why I shall fight wholeheartedly and fearlessly for the future of our republic.

My story actually has its roots centuries ago in Japan.

I've always been drawn to the warrior spirit and the code of the samurai. But it is the ethos of the ronin that truly resonates with me.

During Japan's feudal period, from the late 1100s to the late 1800s, a samurai who lost his lord or master, either through the master's death or the samurai's loss of favor, was known as a ronin. It always struck me as poetic that the word *ronin* translates literally to "wave man"—someone who is adrift.

At the loss of his master, a samurai was bound to commit seppuku, or ritual suicide, according to the Bushido, the code of the samurai. Those who chose not to honor the code were shunned by other samurai and feudal lords as outsiders. In such a rigid social structure, the path chosen by a ronin was not easy, as his desire to serve couldn't be met. Ronin were forbidden to be employed by another master without the previous master's permission.

Despite their outsider status, ronin were permitted to remain armed and carry two swords, but they were barred from employment in a different trade. As a result, some became bodyguards or mercenaries, while others drifted into crime. Regardless, lacking the status or power of honorably employed samurai, ronin were viewed as disreputable and became targets of discrimination. In other words, it was highly undesirable to be a ronin.

So why do I call myself an American ronin?

I lost my own earthly master—my father—early in my life, when I was only twenty-five years old. My father was my ultimate role model.

Herman West Sr. was a warrior himself who served his country in World War II. He raised me to be a strong, principled man, uncompromising in character, and to believe that service to our country was the highest honor.

These same principles were reinforced by my mother, Elizabeth Thomas West. Sadly, my mother died just eight years after my father, in 1994, when I was thirty-three years old.

As a young man without the guidance and loving support of his parents, I could have easily lost my way and eschewed the foundations on which I'd been raised. But like the ronin who continues to carry his swords and practice the way of the warrior, I pledged an oath never to succumb. I vowed to continue in the service of my nation.

And just like the ronin, I have remained an outsider, hewing to the code by which I was raised.

My parents, my earthly masters, had brought me up as a conservative in every sense. They encouraged and championed my commitment to conservative values. Now I stood alone. I soon experienced the ronin's sense of undesirability, humiliation, and shame. I was treated as persona non grata not only by those who didn't share my views but also by some in my own African-American community.

Because I refused to succumb and live my life according to other people's code, I was cast out. But the one thing that continues to burn in me is the desire to live up to the standards of character and excellence taught me by my parents.

This book is a testament to my parents, Buck and Snooks. I hope it serves to strengthen other parents who are raising their own American warriors—warriors who must press on and embody the code and principles their parents impart.

I will strive to explain those principles and the fundamental beliefs of this, our beloved republic, so that all who read these pages will come to respect and honor the American ronin. For we are the ones who continue to live honorably. We are the ones who serve and protect the republic, pledging our swords in the defense of her values, security, and dignity. We are the ones who, in the face of attacks from others, are emboldened to stand stronger and with greater resolve.

I am honored to share the defining moments in my life, my philosophy of governance, an examination of my own black community, and my thoughts on the future of our republic—a republic that now more than ever needs a certain breed: an American ronin.

PART I

MY CONSERVATIVE ROOTS

Chapter 1

EARLY LESSONS

✦ ✦ ✦ ✦ ✦ ✦ ✦ ✦ ✦ ✦ ✦ ✦

*Train up a child in the way he should go; and
when he is old he shall not depart from it.*

—PROVERBS 22:6

I t's March 2013, and I'm looking out over the Caribbean
Sea as waves lap the shores of Grand Cayman. This is
my first visit to the Cayman Islands, and I will certainly
return at some point to dive the famous reef walls.

But my purpose for this trip is to attend the Young
Caymanian Leadership Awards gala this evening as keynote speaker. It's an amazing journey that has brought
me to this place on this day. From the far reaches of Iraq
during Operations Desert Shield and Desert Storm, to the
forbidding terrain of Afghanistan during the early 2000s,
to the storied halls of our nation's capitol in 2011, to this
moment in a fancy hotel in the Caribbean—I never could

have imagined leading such a life given my simple origins in the inner city of Atlanta.

I was born in February 1961. It was a very different America then. Segregation was widely practiced and hotly debated. The possibility of a black president was unimaginable. That summer, a little over six hundred miles south of my hometown, on a beach in Fort Lauderdale, Florida, there was a protest called the "wade-in." A group of civil rights activists joined hands and waded into the whites-only beach off Las Olas Boulevard to protest segregation.

But times do change. Fifty years later, in January 2011, I was sworn in as the United States representative for that very same beach in Florida's Twenty-Second Congressional District.

When considered together, these two seemingly unrelated events—a wade-in and a man pledging the oath of office—testify to the exceptionalism of our republic, the same type of exceptionalism that my parents instilled in me from a young age.

When I was growing up, my mother taught me a simple maxim: "A man must stand for something or he will fall for anything." That sentiment may well have guided a young man born a bastard on the island of Nevis in the British West Indies not far from Grand Cayman, where I am writing this book today. Somehow this young man made it to a place where he could seek his own destiny. He fought in the Continental Army for the independence of a fledgling country soon to be called the United States. He became a member of the Continental Congress. He was a cowriter of what must be considered the greatest political document ever written, the Constitution of the United States. Ultimately he became the first secretary of the treasury of America. His name was Alexander Hamilton.

America is indeed a great land of dreams and opportunity. This fact is as true today as it was in the time of Alexander Hamilton.

In my case, my opportunity—and indeed my destiny—was to uphold this republic, first by serving in the military and then by serving in government. As an American ronin, I hold steadfast to my beliefs, no matter what challenges or obstacles arise in my path. In 2012 I sought reelection to the US House of Representatives in the newly drawn Eighteenth Congressional District in southeastern Florida. To say the campaign was hotly contested would be a gross understatement. I remember being in the city of Port Saint Lucie at an early-voting site when a black woman came up to me. She asked if I was Allen West. I don't know how she could have been unsure about that, but in any event, I knew from her tone of voice what was about to follow—and she didn't let me down.

As my fellow black American looked at me, her face began to distort and she screamed, "How could you do this? How could you be one of *them*? Your parents are ashamed of you. You are not a real black person."

My response? Just a smile, a simple smile, because this woman was forgetting completely the best aspect of America: free will. Obviously she didn't understand that I am, and continue to be, exactly what my parents raised me to be. As Solomon said in the book of Proverbs, "train up a child in the way he should go"—in other words, our lives are shaped by our early lessons, and I was fortunate to have parents who taught me to exercise freedom of thought.

I was the middle son of Herman and Elizabeth Thomas West. My parents were affectionately nicknamed Buck and Snooks, and for the sake of this book, that's how I will refer to them from now on—even though they would've whupped me silly if they ever heard me call them that.

I never knew my grandmothers. They both passed before I was born. My granddads were Jule Wynn on my father's side and Samuel Thomas on my mother's, and both were rocks of men. My grandfathers had soft-spoken demeanors, but they commanded respect and admiration for their comportment and wisdom. As a child I loved going down south to Cuthbert, Georgia, to visit Granddad Jule. Granddad Sam lived over in southeast Atlanta. You could see Lakewood Stadium and the fairgrounds from his backyard. I also spent lots of time visiting my Aunt Madear down in Camilla, Georgia. From these wise men and women, I learned to cultivate the cornerstone of character: respect. Often I would simply sit and listen to them tell their stories, but they also demanded that I talk to them and tell them about my life. Nowadays children are allowed to stay absorbed in their keypads and headphones, but I was taught at an early age how to communicate, listen respectfully, and appreciate the insights of my elders.

They'd take me fishing or out to pick pecans (properly pronounced in southern vernacular as PEE-cans) or peaches (to this day I don't like peaches because of the incessant itching caused by peach fuzz). Sometimes they'd have me walk with them to local stores and make me carry the bags—a practice that today is sadly considered "old school."

Madear and both granddads have gone on, but I will never forget Granddad Jule's description of me as a young kid. He told my father, "Buck, that boy Allen of yours is as stubborn as a mule sometimes, but he is a good boy."

My dad, Buck West, was born in 1920 in Ozark, Alabama, but he somehow managed to jump the Chattahoochee River over to Georgia, where he grew up. Dad stood about five feet eleven inches and wore a flattop high and tight—which is why I wear the same haircut to this day. Buck was a soft-spoken but direct man, loved by all with whom he came in contact. His word was his bond, and you could always count on him. Dad served in World War II as a logistics specialist. I was enraptured by his stories of North Africa during a time of war, of the Anzio beach landing in Italy, and of the time he went to Rome and saw the Vatican.

Dad was wounded in Italy during a Nazi bombardment. He had been running dispatches on a motorcycle (now you know why I ride). He experienced severe head trauma and remained in a coma for a spell. I'll never forget the first time he allowed me to touch the bumps left on his head.

Dad came back to America and met and married his first wife. They had my older brother, Herman West Jr., whom we all knew by the nickname "Pootney." Unfortunately Dad's first wife passed away, but he eventually met my mom. Rumor has it they were really good dancers— but I can assure you that's one area where I don't take after Buck West! Dad worked as an insurance agent for a time but eventually, after marrying my mom, got a job with the Veterans Administration hospital in Atlanta.

My mother, Snooks West, was born in 1931 in south Georgia. I'm unclear about the geographic particulars— she was born in the vicinity of Fort Valley and Perry, but she spent time growing up around Camilla. For me, Fort Valley was her home and where the folks on my mother's side lived.

Both my parents had relatives in the Albany-Camilla-Thomasville area of Georgia. As a young kid, I thought my mom's family had founded Thomasville, since Thomas was her maiden name. Mom went to Fort Valley State

College and was a public school teacher for quite some time. As it happens, my high school girlfriend's mother had been taught by my mother (and yeah, that made for some awkward moments).

Mom and Dad moved to Atlanta sometime around 1959 and found a home in the historic Fourth Ward. They bought a nice two-story house at 651 Kennesaw Avenue Northeast, a small street between Ponce de Leon Avenue and North Avenue. The house is still there, and whenever I'm in Atlanta, I go by and relive memories. My mom's younger brother and sister, Uncle Sam and Aunt Brendalyn, also lived in our house and were like older siblings to me.

Our small street was a little oasis of families, two-parent homes, kids, and a real sense of community. In those days the treat for us youngsters was playing street ball while the old men sat by the sidewalk, told stories, and watched over us, warning us of oncoming cars. As we grew older, we would go to friends' houses to watch the old men play checkers. If you want excitement, watch a group of older gents compete at checkers like we did. I truly believe that their banter was the genesis of trash talking.

Our neighborhood included the Heards, Jacksons, Rowes, Martins, Davenports, Littles, and Washingtons. While the men played checkers, the women would sit out on the porches and talk. There were times when the old men would let one of us young ones step up to the checkers table. They knew it wouldn't take long to smash us, and it didn't. Most times I remember them spanking us in about four moves. Bam! And it was over. Then, of course, came the trash talking to our dads about not teaching us to play—but at least teaching us how to take a whipping.

Back then there was no hiring folks to cut your grass or wash the car. We young fellas developed a sense of business by competing against each other for grass-cutting and car-washing jobs. I learned about pricing and providing services in the free market at an early age. You could cut grass, but then someone would undercut you by offering lawn edging. You could wash a car, but some-one would also offer to sweep the inside and give the in-terior a good leather shine. Success was about competing for and getting the job and then doing it so well that you were the one in demand. My angle was to tackle the big jobs, such as the backyards where the kudzu vines grew. And that's how I spent my Saturdays growing up—grass cutting and car washing.

On Sunday there was only one place you were going to be, and that was church. Several churches stood proudly all along "our" Boulevard. My family's church was Fort Street United Methodist Church, where I also attended Sunday school. Every Sunday the nine a.m. parade of residents would leave from our little street, cross North Avenue, and head over to Boulevard, where we'd stop off at our respective houses of worship.

Church was where you made your other group of friends, especially for me, because many people in our congregation came from all across the Atlanta area. Only severe sickness could get you out of church. Even if you were visiting extended family elsewhere, you were not going to miss Sunday services. When I stayed with relatives down in south Georgia, I was *certainly* going to church—no way was I going to embarrass my mom and dad by not attending.

But it wasn't just the weekly sermons and Sunday school lessons that taught me the fundamental principles of faith. I remember the ol' "Mothers of the Church." Trust me, in church everyone was your mother—in fact these ladies were allowed to smack you. The elders of the church were my surrogate dads. Disrespecting them at times could be worse than disrespecting my own father.

Back in the old-school way, a child was an extension of the parents. The child reflected the parents and their parenting skills, and you as the child were their calling card. I remember being down in Cuthbert and going out somewhere. When I was walking back to my granddad's, I didn't speak to any of the folks sitting out on the front porches. I had no sooner hit Granddad's first step when my dad greeted me with a whack. It had already gotten back to him that his boy Allen was disrespectful and did not properly greet his elders.

Buck was a quiet man, and I learned never to have a negative effect on his impeccable reputation, especially in his hometown. You can bet from that moment on, I learned to say *good morning, good day, good afternoon, good evening, sir, ma'am*—and that lesson resonates with me today. In fact, it's a courtesy I demand my own daughters practice.

Mom was the real disciplinarian in our home. I saw Snooks West as a benevolent dictator, and I mean she was *tough*. Mom was an old-school southern woman with a soft, sweet voice and dialect. She stood around five feet six inches but had a demeanor that made her seem six feet tall. She was the standard-bearer, and she demanded excellence. Dad and Mom had separate bedrooms, but they loved each other. It was just that Mom, as the ultimate independent woman, wanted her space. Truth be told, Mom was a tad bit, well, messy. But she was a first-class woman and loved to dress, and it's no surprise that her closet was always overflowing.

Mom was thrifty, however, and she never believed in owing anyone. Her favorite place to shop was Sears, Roebuck, which was right down the street on Ponce de Leon. Remember layaway? That was Mom's preferred means to get something she wanted. And she was not about to overspend. Instead she would set the money aside, little by little.

When Mom went to get herself a new car, she paid in cash. She would go to the dealership and find what she wanted. When the sales guy asked about payment plans,

Mom would softly say, "How much is the price, child?" and proceed to write a check.

My dad was equally thrifty. I found it hard to believe how incredibly savvy my mom and dad were with finances. They were careful investors and could make a dollar stretch like you cannot imagine. If they were on Capitol Hill today, our federal budget would be balanced easily.

Because of their belief in fiscal responsibility and their deep-seated desire to make a better life for subsequent generations, they invested in education for me and later for my younger brother, Arlan. They knew that the key to our futures was having a good education, for it is the great equalizer and the means by which the playing field is truly leveled. Even before starting elementary school, I was attending private tutoring sessions, which gave me a tremendous head start. I knew how to write cursive before the first grade (which is why I cannot print worth a doggone now!). When it came time for me to enter grammar school, Mom and Dad were not going to have me subjected to a substandard school system. So they enrolled me at a private Catholic school, Our Lady of Lourdes, at the intersection of Boulevard and Auburn Avenue. There I would be educated in the shadows of the famous Ebenezer Baptist Church and across the street from the memorial and gravesite of Dr. Martin Luther King Jr.

It is the parents, not the government, who are primarily responsible for their children's education, and my mom and dad comprehended that. They also understood that parents should have choices for where their children attend school.

Today my wife, Angela, and I also realize the importance of educational choice, and we have made investment in our daughters' education our highest priority. I believe a solid foundation of learning is critical to ensure greater opportunities for the next generation, our children and grandchildren. My folks sacrificed so that I could attend a private Catholic school, and I will never forget their generosity and selflessness.

I finished at Our Lady of Lourdes in the seventh grade. After that, Mom wanted me to attend a larger private school, and she set her sights on Westminster, Lovett, Pace Academy, or Marist. I took the entrance exam for Marist and made the cut—it didn't hurt that I was a decent athlete.

I entered eighth grade at Marist School with some excitement. At the time Marist was an independent Catholic day school and had about seven hundred students, all boys. It was an academic and athletic powerhouse. Even baseball star Hank Aaron's sons, Hank Jr. and Larry, attended that school.

For the first time in my young life, however, I began to feel the burdens of stress and pressure. I had to get up early to catch the first bus running to downtown and then hop on the transfer bus to Ashford Dunwoody Road, where Marist was located. I was playing sports, which meant really late nights getting home.

On top of everything else, out of the seven hundred students at Marist, only seven were black. I'd only recently left Our Lady of Lourdes, a black inner-city Catholic school, and now everything was turned upside down. It was becoming harder to relate to my friends on Kennesaw Avenue, and the heckling on the bus coming home was getting worse. I did well in eighth grade, but the pressure started taking its toll in ninth. I needed a change.

And for the first time ever, simple, quiet Allen—who had always done what everyone wanted—now asked to be heard. I begged my mom to let me transfer to Grady High, the local public school just down the street. Mom refused to listen, so in the early days of 1976, I began to plan.

I knew I had to do something to show my mom I was serious about changing schools. I decided I would run away to my Aunt Sally in Alexandria, Virginia. I studied the Greyhound schedules and found a bus that departed early morning for Washington, DC. I began to pay attention to my dad's nighttime habits and time his trips to the bathroom. When walking down the stairs in our house, I noted which steps creaked.

Dad had a huge mayonnaise jar of quarters, and I often donated to the jar to keep change handy. I began to increase my donations from my weekend chores so that this kitty would fund my escape. It was an intricate plan, and it had to be executed to perfection or else. Perhaps that's why to this day I love the movies *The Great Escape* and *Von Ryan's Express*.

Finally the night came when I was ready. I went to bed fully dressed. I borrowed my older brother's ivory-handled bayonet from Vietnam for protection, snatched a blue denim jacket, and eased downstairs, carefully paying attention to where I stepped on the stairs. I grabbed the quarter jar, gently opened the door, and was off.

I had left a message on my bed so my folks wouldn't worry about where I was heading. Now, in the middle of the night, I made my way off Kennesaw Avenue to North Avenue and was spotted by an Atlanta Police Department patrol car. I knew the officers would double back. So I took an alternate route and evaded the patrol. I reached the Greyhound station in downtown Atlanta about fifteen minutes before the bus was scheduled to depart. The ticket agent stood there and watched while I counted out the fare in quarters. I boarded the bus and took a seat in the back. I was free!

A day later I arrived in Washington, DC, and made my way to Aunt Sally's house, where she and my Uncle Bill were waiting. I spent about four days at Aunt Sally's, and Mom finally understood my concerns. I flew back to Atlanta, and boy howdy, was I nervous. What would happen when I got home? Well, Dad was at the airport to meet me, and he gave me a hug. He looked at me and said in his strong Buck West voice, "Boy, I am proud of you for standing up and showing you have some spunk in you. I have always wondered if you would ever make a rebellious act, and you did, but you did it responsibly. However, if you ever do something like that again, I will kill you." Mom, well, she was a bit of a mess. She was crying and felt like a failure. I told her she wasn't, it was just that I needed her to listen to me.

The real challenge was going back to Marist and finishing the remainder of ninth grade. Some people looked at me differently because I'd run away from home. But something important had happened. The whole episode had been liberating. It showed me that there are times when I need to make a stand and not be concerned with what others feel or believe. It was a major turning point in my life. And thus later that year I became a sophomore at Henry Grady High.

I flourished at Grady. I quickly developed leadership skills, and I received the rank of cadet lieutenant in my first year of Army Junior Reserve Officers' Training Corps. I worked out with the varsity football team and was made captain of the junior team. During my junior year, I became cadet/lieutenant colonel battalion commander above those who were seniors, and I made the varsity track team. In my senior year, I was copresident of the student body and won awards at several math contests. When I graduated Grady High, I received the

1979 Atlanta Journal-Constitution Cup for the Best All-Around Senior.

My parents had accepted my stance, but in turn I stepped up and took responsibility and ownership for what I'd done. I worked part-time jobs to make sure I could buy my own clothes—there were no more boring blue shirts, ties, blazers, and gray or khaki pants for me. I showed friends that I was part of the neighborhood, but I still maintained a sense of excellence and the highest academic standards.

The decision to change schools had opened up more leadership opportunities than I could have imagined. I was now on my way to college.

My homeroom teacher at Grady, Ms. Carolyn Payne, had the greatest influence on my selection of college. My choice had come down to either North Georgia College in Dahlonega or the University of Tennessee in Knoxville, which Ms. Payne had attended, and she explained why her alma mater was so great and the right fit for me. I knew my parents' dream was for me to become an officer in the military. My older brother was a Marine, and Mom now worked at a Marine Corps headquarters, but I wanted be a soldier like my dad. So it was the US Army for me. Because Tennessee had one of the best ROTC programs in the country, the choice was UT. Furthermore, my Aunt Bren and my two cousins lived in Knoxville.

By the time my parents dropped me off at Hess Hall

on the Tennessee campus, they had fully prepared me to take wing and fly. The question then became, would I depart from the principles and standards they'd worked so hard to teach me? There were to be bumps along the road, as is true of any journey. But today as I write these words, gazing out on the Caribbean and listening to folks enjoy the sun and surf, I can honestly say I've stayed true to the principles of Buck and Snooks.

They instilled in me a sense of faith, family, and God. They enabled me to appreciate service to our country. They taught me about fiscal responsibility, the quality of a good education, and personal responsibility. They showed me what it was like to be strong yet caring. They had raised a man, an American ronin, who would dedicate his life to being a guardian of the republic.

Buck West passed in 1986 of a massive stroke. He died in the same VA hospital where he worked to comfort our veterans. Years earlier, when I would visit him at his job, I learned about those men and women who had once been willing to give that last full measure of devotion. Dad was a faithful man, but not a religious one. In general he didn't trust those "ol' rascal ministers." I remember the first time he ever attended Fort Street United Methodist Church: it was when I was home from Italy on leave. The next time he entered that church was the day we bade him farewell.

Snooks West passed in 1994, succumbing to liver cancer. Because of her more than twenty-five years of civilian service to the US military as a transportation coordinator for the Marine Corps, she was given military honors. She had been a faithful and involved member of Fort Street Church, even singing in the choir. At their funerals both Mom and Dad had a church full of folks who had come to say good-bye because my parents were so loved and respected. After all these years, thinking of their deaths still brings tears to my eyes.

At Mom's funeral I held our first daughter, Aubrey. She was nine months old. The pastor addressed the congregation and eulogized Snooks by referring to a woman who had raised three men. She had certainly done that, but her reach was far greater.

If you are ever up at Marietta National Cemetery, you will see that Buck and Snooks lie together, with one headstone, one grave. As they were in life, so they shall be in death. Man and woman, husband and wife, Dad and Mom, Buck and Snooks. I hope they rest peacefully, knowing I have not departed from their ways.

Chapter 2

SHAPING OPERATIONS

★ ★ ★ ★ ★ ★ ★ ★ ★ ★ ★ ★ ★

*Be all you can be. Find your future in the
Army.*

—US Army slogan

I t was the marketing motto that would shape my life:
BAYCB, "Be all you can be." Right up there with "You
deserve a break today" and "I'd like to buy the world
a Coke," it was one of the best-known advertising jin-
gles in America. So doggone, why did some chucklehead
come up with that "Army of One" foolishness?

In military vernacular there are two types of operations: decisive and shaping. Before any decisive operation,
there must be a shaping operation to set the conditions
for the final attack and to ensure victory is achieved and
objectives are met.

My military career was the shaping operation that made me the man I am today.

Throughout the history of our nation, there have always been those patriots who served in uniform and then went on to greater service of our country. To quote an oft-debated question, I ask you, "Are leaders born or made?" I tend to believe leaders are made. They are shaped through a progression of experiences and circumstances that inspire something in them to rise above the occasion.

One of my favorite leaders in American history is a simple man who answered the call to arms and who stood as a giant at a moment when the future of our country was in peril. Such was the story of one American, a professor of rhetoric at Bowdoin College in Maine. His expertise was language, not combat arms or the science of warfare. However, when our country was torn in two and challenged in battle, and when the fundamental premise on which America had been established was being threatened, Joshua Lawrence Chamberlain answered the call.

During the Civil War, one of his first major engagements was at the Battle of Fredericksburg, Virginia. There he led a futile charge across the field toward Marye's Heights. All through the night he was pinned down against sniper fire, and without a doubt that experience and loss shaped him as a developing combat leader.

It was not long after the Fredericksburg engagement

that Chamberlain's Twentieth Maine Volunteer Infantry Regiment, as part of the Army of the Potomac, found itself marching north to a road junction at a place in Pennsylvania called Gettysburg. Word had been received that General Robert E. Lee's Army of Northern Virginia had crossed in behind the Blue Ridge, had entered Pennsylvania, and was turning south.

On the first day there, Brigadier General John Buford's cavalry dismounted and held the high ground along Cemetery Ridge for the Union, enabling fellow Union General George Meade's main force to close and reinforce. Buford's delay would be one of the greatest actions in US military history, an incredible shaping action that would set the conditions for the decisive action on day three of the Battle of Gettysburg.

It was on day two, however—a hot July day in 1863—that Colonel Chamberlain found himself in a precarious position at the far end of the Union line, which extended all the way back to Gettysburg and almost curved back on itself like a fishhook. It was there where Chamberlain was given orders that he could not retreat, could not withdraw, and must hold the ground. Little did Chamberlain know, but the primary effort of the Confederates that day would be against that same far Union flank, with General John Bell Hood leading the assault.

After the Confederates fought through the rocky crags of Devil's Den, they turned their sights on what would become known as Little Round Top, where Chamberlain's depleted Twentieth Maine Regiment waited. The assault came in wave after wave against the Maine men, and soon casualties were rising, ammunition was running low, and a sense of panic was growing. As Chamberlain saw the Confederate forces turning their flank, he managed to extend coverage in a maneuver called "refuse the line." But eventually the Maine regiment's ammunition ran out, and the Confederate men of the Twentieth Alabama Infantry Regiment prepared for another charge against the Union forces.

Chamberlain, wounded in the leg, gave an order that had never been given in the Union Army. He "ordered the bayonet" and, using a maneuver called a "swinging gate," created a frontal assault and flanking attack simultaneously, leading the charge that saved the day at Little Round Top.

With his actions, Chamberlain saved the Union Army of the Potomac. He saved Gettysburg and the North from the Army of Northern Virginia. And above all he saved the Union.

The bookish professor of rhetoric from Maine was later awarded the Medal of Honor and was given the privilege of accepting General Robert E. Lee's sword at Appomattox Court House, ending the Civil War. Chamberlain, a Republican, returned home to Maine, where he served several terms as governor.

Colonel, governor, and professor, Joshua Lawrence Chamberlain rose to the occasion. He answered that call to service and never stopped serving even after his days in uniform were over. He was the rare man who will stand among the greatest of military and civilian leaders in America. He truly embodied the slogan "Be all you can be."

My journey to "be all I could be" started in the US Army Junior Reserve Officers' Training Corps (JROTC) program at Henry Grady High School. I always knew I wanted to join the US Army. From hearing my dad's stories of World War II, and from meeting Marines at my mom's workplace, I knew my destiny was the military. It was Mom and Dad who said they wanted the first officer in the family. And now, as it happens, we have our second officer, my nephew Major Herman Bernard West III. Doggone, I remember bouncing that fella on my knee. . . .

This is how a family legacy of service is established. This is how a nation shall always be protected, because each generation inspires and raises the next generation of guardians.

At Grady High I came to know esteemed warriors who would shape me into the soldier and man I am today. These men—Lieutenant Colonel Pagonis, Major Heredia, Master Sergeant Buchanan, and Sergeant First Class McMichael—had served in Korea and Vietnam. Master Sergeant Buchanan had been a prisoner of war. He told horrific stories and showed us student cadets his arm, which had been debilitated during his time in captivity. Major Heredia spoke of the Korean War and of the Chinese and North Korean tactics of using captured Americans to force tank columns to stop and be ambushed. I learned that there was evil in this world that must be confronted and that our country needed men and women willing to stand as watchmen on the ramparts of freedom and liberty. As former combat leaders, my ROTC instructors had decided, much as Joshua Lawrence Chamberlain and others before them, to continue serving the nation through their local community. I firmly believe the Army JROTC program plays a vital role in developing the United States' future leaders, because it exposes students to men and women who have been leaders and servants of our republic. I'm honored to receive many speaking invitations, but I truly love those opportunities to address high school JROTC cadets, because that program gave me my start.

My instructors at Grady High saw something in me that I didn't know existed: leadership potential. They selected me to be the program battalion commander when I was a junior. Now, that did cause some angst among the seniors, but they knew I'd earned the privilege. And because I'd learned to concern myself more with being respected than liked, it all worked out. We had a fantastic battalion. During my year as commander, we earned our gold star designation as one of the top Army JROTC programs in Atlanta among more than twenty high schools.

Those men—Pagonis, Heredia, Buchanan, and

McMichael—taught me pride in wearing the uniform, they enhanced my sense of discipline, and they imparted to me a burning desire to be an Army officer. Those men were like an extension of my dad. They had "that way" about them. When it was ROTC day to serve as cafeteria monitors, doggone, was it orderly. All they had to do was give that look and even the "baddest of the bad" would pipe down. When Sergeant McMichael got steamed at you, boy, could he break you down.

Now there are people who would take programs like high school JROTC out of schools. Frankly I believe they are misguided idiots who have no clue that what they're doing could actually harm our young people. If ever I were to become US president, I'd ensure that every inner-city high school had a JROTC program.

When I left Grady, I was ready to join the ROTC program at the University of Tennessee. Because I had three years of high school ROTC under my belt, I was fast-tracked to begin working on my commission as an Army officer. But as I mentioned, there are always bumps in the road, and I hit my first one in college. I was put on academic probation in my sophomore year and suspended from the ROTC program. Here I was, so close to the one thing I truly wanted in life—to be an Army second lieutenant—and I had nearly blown it. For a moment I toyed with the idea of dropping out of college and working, but that thought didn't last long. I knew I had to knuckle down.

First things first, I wanted to move off campus.

I lived in the Hess Hall dorm during my freshman year and in Clement Hall in my second. Now, for my junior year, I found a nice one-bedroom place for 180 bucks a month. Mom and Dad said they were not going to pay for an apartment. Frankly they were pissed off about my grades. It wasn't that I was spending time partying or hanging out, I just hadn't found my academic path.

I'd gone to college thinking I wanted to be an engineer. I spent a year and a half in that major, and Statics and Dynamics just about did me in. I loved math, but I wasn't an abstract thinker. So I switched my major to political science. The summer before my junior year, I got my old job back at Sears in the Columbia Mall in DeKalb County and worked my butt off to save up money for the apartment. Ol' Buck recognized how I was busting my butt, and he chipped in for some furniture. Little did I realize that my apartment would become *his* weekend getaway with my little brother, Arlan, especially during college football season! During my junior year, I took a couple of jobs as night desk watchman at a dorm and salesclerk at a music store called the Record Bar and showed the folks I could take charge of my life.

Just like my high school decision and plan to run away, the way I chose to embark on my junior year at UT reflected another life-changing choice. I restored my grades and was reinstated in the ROTC program. And thus, during the summer of 1982, I found myself flying off to Fort Lewis, Washington, for summer Advanced Camp, a boot camp for ROTC students seeking to earn a commission. Little did I know it then, but years later I would return to Fort Lewis as an instructor and evaluate cadets in those very same barracks.

Advanced Camp was long at seven weeks, and back in the day it was tough. The nights in the Pacific Northwest were damn cold, especially for this southern boy. It was always wet, and I had never seen mosquitoes that bad! I ended up getting quite sick and was coughing up blood at one point, but I was not about to quit or be recycled. This was it. I had completed all of my ROTC requirements. All I had to do was complete Advanced Camp and I would be Second Lieutenant Allen B. West.

Well, I finished, and on graduation day I was ecstatic. I'd met friends who would be my colleagues for years to come. I flew from Fort Lewis back to Atlanta, and there was Buck waiting with this huge smile on his face. He looked at me and how skinny I was and said, "They kicked your butt, didn't they, boy?"

I was always going to be his boy. Years earlier he'd gone to the airport to collect his boy who'd run away; now he was picking up soon-to-be "2LT" West. The entire family traveled to Knoxville for the big day. It was July 31, 1982, and my parents and brothers watched me take the oath—the third member of our family to do so—giving my pledge to "support and defend the Constitution of the United States against all enemies foreign

33

and domestic, and bear true faith and allegiance to the same."

What a day. What a special honor. I was on top of the world. I still needed to complete my academic requirements at Tennessee, which I did the following summer. I couldn't believe it: I was Second Lieutenant Allen B. West with a bachelor's degree in political science. You had to pinch me.

I returned to Atlanta and worked at Sears while awaiting my order to active duty. Then the orders arrived, and I was instructed to report to Fort Sill, Oklahoma, for Field Artillery Officer Basic Course, class 2-84. Before I departed, Buck and Pootney sat me on the front steps and gave me the lecture I surely needed. These were the words that stuck in my mind from these two combat veterans: "You are a brand-new, fresh second lieutenant. You don't know nothing and need to come to that realization. You need to find your platoon sergeant and listen to him. Make sure you allow him to teach you. He will respect you because of the rank, but he needs to respect you as a man and leader. Never forget that if you take care of your soldiers, your men, they will take care of you and hold you in high esteem and respect. Screw your men over, and they will screw you over. A good leader is first a good follower. Listen and lead, but most of all, take care of your men."

Those parting words would guide me some twenty-two years later to make a spontaneous decision on the battlefield in Iraq, one that would have an indelible impact on my life. But more on that later in this chapter. The trip to Fort Sill was my first time driving to this part of the country. Entering Key Gate, I was at the home of the Field Artillery, a truly historic place, and one now part of my history. The six months at Fort Sill were something special. I was introduced to the Army culture.

I was also introduced to the precision of gunnery and shoots. Since I was passionate about math, gunnery was especially fun for me. Others hated it, but I really got into the old-school calculations using slide rules and charts to solve problems. In fact, some of the other fellas would come to me for gunnery tutoring before exams. Having to devise gunnery firing solutions was awesome, and the shoots . . . well, sitting on a hilltop striving to put an artillery round within fifty meters of the target was challenging, especially in an Oklahoma winter. Crap, I had never been that cold. And don't forget, these were the days before Gore-Tex and all that high-tech, high-end gear. My follow-on orders came for the Second Infantry Division in Korea. I didn't mind. If I was to excel in my trade, I wanted to be where there was an adversary, and that was certainly true in 1984 in Korea with its demilitarized zone.

Without my knowledge, however, my name was also submitted—and selected—for an Airborne unit in Vicenza, Italy. Airborne? Jumping out of airplanes? Doggone, now that was a bit of a surprise. Our TAC (training, advising, and counseling) officer told me I had been chosen because of my class standing, physical fitness level—back then I could run like the wind—and sharpness.

So from Fort Sill, I came home to Georgia for Basic Airborne Course. I was roster number A114 in Airborne School and I successfully graduated, but then came the real challenge. With only five jumps under my belt, I was supposed to pass one of the toughest schools in the Army, Jumpmaster School. I was adopted by an Airborne instructor who took a liking to me, and after two weeks of intense training, studying, and written and hands-on exams, I passed. I was off to Italy. Before I left I married my college sweetheart, Gail Mosby, in a small, intimate ceremony at Fort Benning. Gail had been a strong Christian influence in my life and was instrumental in keeping me focused.

In Italy I was assigned to the 509th Parachute Infantry Battalion, which was soon designated as the Fourth Battalion, 325th Infantry Regiment. This was the perfect unit for an officer beginning his service. I had many memorable experiences during my Vicenza assignment. I learned to ski, and, before redeploying, I was even the winter training base camp OIC (officer in charge). The moment that began my political maturity, however, came in the winter of 1985 when I went through Checkpoint Charlie into East Berlin. President Ronald Reagan had given his famous "evil empire" speech in 1983, and during that winter I saw the reality of communism and socialism and the importance of President Reagan's words. I walked the streets with Soviet officers and soldiers as well as East Germans. I saw the plight, the lack of freedom, and the emptiness in the eyes of the people. Right then I understood what makes America exceptional. I also recognized that there was indeed an ideological enemy, and I didn't ever want to live under its thumb. I came to understand what freedom and liberty meant and why it was worth fighting for. When Reagan bombed Libya, we soldiers all felt a sense of pride that we were fighting back. The malaise of Jimmy Carter was gone. We were soldiers at a turning point, and we knew it.

During the tour of duty in Italy, Gail and I suffered several traumas—the loss of her mom and the loss of my dad. It had been a tough assignment for a young new lieutenant who left his wife nine months out of the year while deploying all across Europe on contingency missions. I was not a good husband, nor ready to be one. By the time I returned from Italy we had separated, and in 1988, we divorced. We maintained a healthy friendship over the years, and in 1994 she was there for my mom's funeral.

And so in 1987 I faced a difficult trip back across the country for Field Artillery Officer Advanced Course. Emotionally, I was starting over. For the first time in my life, I had not seen something through.

After the course I was reassigned to Fort Riley in Kansas. I had asked for Fort Benning, Fort Stewart, or Fort

Campbell, as I had thoughts of resigning my commission after this second tour and wanted to be back down south. Coming from an Airborne unit, now heading to a Mechanized Division, First Infantry, I didn't know what to expect. The assignment ended up being a blessing, because I met a man who would be a great friend and mentor for many years—Colonel John R. Gingrich, aka Da G-Man. I was recommended for early battery command. Again I jumped ahead of peers and senior captains. Yep, I was a captain now.

My professional career was thriving, but I felt empty emotionally. Then God sent an angel my way. Her name, fittingly enough, was Angela. Her dad had been a career military man, and she was completing her MBA at Long Island University in Brooklyn. Somehow I convinced her to marry me and come back to Manhattan, Kansas, where she had been an undergrad at Kansas State University. Naturally I was concerned about being a better husband and man, and I'm still working on that today.

No sooner had we been married than a little something kicked up far away in a place called Kuwait. Colonel Gingrich chose me to lead the advance party for the battalion, and I left my new bride not knowing what the future would hold. I had experienced the ideological evil of communism and socialism in my first duty assignment in Europe. I was now about to experience the evil of a Middle Eastern dictatorship.

We routed the Iraqi army in no time, maybe a hundred hours. We were just that good at open desert warfare. I had been to the National Training Center in the Mojave Desert several times and knew my trade as a fire support officer very well.

However, once our major combat operations were over and we had pounded the enemy, something struck me hard. An Iraqi woman found her way into our headquarters base camp. She was dehydrated and had her children with her. Soldiers in the Iraqi army had raped her and killed her husband and brother. We quickly got her medical support, but that level of brutality was something my colleagues and I discussed long after. Now I was learning about another type of evil, and I became interested in reading about and understanding Muslim culture in a historical and contemporary context so that I could make sense of what I had seen.

Operations Desert Shield and Desert Storm were awesome experiences for a young captain, but afterward I witnessed the mistake we always seem to repeat in America. We drew down our forces to reduce defense spending and made the military pay the bills for other government programs. I headed over to Kansas State to teach ROTC, where Angela was a professor in the business college.

At Kansas State I was responsible for training cadets during their most important junior year to prepare them for their officer boot camp. Coincidentally they would attend the same Fort Lewis Advanced Camp that I had trained at back in the summer of 1982. We were very successful at K-State and created what would become one of the best ROTC programs in the nation. In 1994 I was honored to be named the Army ROTC Instructor of the Year. Many of the former cadets are now senior majors, lieutenant colonels, and even battalion commanders, and we still keep in touch. One of my cadets was part of the Special Forces unit that first went into Afghanistan fighting on horseback with the Northern Alliance against the Taliban.

At the same time that I was training cadets, I was working on my first master's degree. In 1995, after our daughter Aubrey was born and I had completed my academic work, I received a one-year assignment to Korea, the place I was originally supposed to have been sent in 1984.

So off to Korea I went, to the Second Infantry Division as an operations planner and assistant operations officer in the Division Support Command—a great assignment. I was promoted to major there and selected for the Army Staff College back in Kansas.

In Korea I saw evil once again. Standing on the demilitarized zone—the DMZ—and looking into North Korea, I could see the totalitarian Stalinist state. Through my studies and education, I grew to understand these various governing philosophies and how they contrasted with that of our American republic. I knew one day we would have to confront North Korea because the world vision of its leaders is antithetical to our own. Sadly, as I write this in 2013, it seems that day may be drawing closer. Nonetheless, for me it was an incredible experience to have been behind the Iron Curtain and to stand guard along the DMZ. My worldview continued to develop.

I returned to the States. Between 1996 and 1997, I completed work on two master's degrees and graduated from Army Staff College. Our second daughter, Austen, arrived and I received orders for a new assignment at Fort Bragg. I would be working for my next great teacher, coach, mentor, and friend—Colonel Denny R. Lewis, incoming commander of the Eighteenth Field Artillery Brigade (Airborne).

This was the largest artillery unit in the Army. Colonel Lewis selected a brand-new staff college graduate and major—me—to be his operations officer. He was hard as woodpecker lips in the winter, but also brilliant and laser-focused. Serving under this gentleman set me on a course to be an exceptional leader, trainer, and manager of resources. One day when we were sitting in the backseat of his command Hummer discussing his vision of a battalion evaluation exercise, Colonel Lewis gave me the simplest order in my military career: "Al, don't screw this up." Truth be told, he used more colorful language than that. My time with Colonel Lewis at Fort Bragg played a tremendous role in shaping me into the leader I am today, which I'll discuss more in the following chapter.

After serving as the colonel's operations officer (OpsO), I was reassigned in the brigade to be the executive officer of the First Battalion (Air Assault), 377th Field Artillery Regiment. I was now second in command of a battalion—the little kid from the inner city of Atlanta, Buck and Snooks's son. And I have to say, my radio call sign was freakin' awesome: Gunslinger 5! The highlight there was a two-month deployment to Alaska to test a new artillery munition called Sense and Destroy Armor (SADARM).

I was the Task Force Gunslinger Gators commander. Due to the exceptional gunnery skills of our unit, especially our Alpha Battery, we were able to uncover serious issues with that munition and its ability to accurately read meteorological, or met, data. Accurate met data readings are needed at the firing-unit location for the target area, but when target-area met data deviated greatly from the firing unit, the munition was not very effective. Because of our efforts, the Army and Marine Corps realized significant savings by not fielding this flawed munition. We didn't just want to be good artillerymen, we also wanted to be good stewards of taxpayers' dollars.

Not long after returning from Alaska, I got word about the next assignment: a joint exchange to the United States Marine Corps at Marine Corps Base Camp Lejuene. Heck, I thought I must have pissed off someone in the Army to get that, but the three-year assignment was one of the best in my career. I made friendships that have transcended time and distance. I was reintroduced to the spirit of the warrior, and my toughness was challenged and strengthened. I was treated just like a Marine staff officer. It was great.

Two seriously traumatic events occurred during this tour. First, Angela was diagnosed with breast cancer. She fought hard and is in complete remission today, but there were dicey moments. From her and through that experience, I learned what real toughness is. I am so very proud of her.

The other traumatic event affected not only my family but our entire nation. It was September 11, 2001—the Pearl Harbor of my generation. As soldiers, we knew America would call upon us, and we had to be ready. I'd studied Muslim culture and had come to understand the radical Islamic terrorist mentality. While Islamic totalitarianism was something seemingly new to many, it has threatened our culture for some time. Thomas Jefferson fought it, in the form of the Barbary pirates, and now this enemy had stepped out of the pages of history and had attacked our shores.

I would not deploy to Afghanistan or Iraq with my Marine brothers and sisters. Instead I was promoted to lieutenant colonel in the Army in 2001 and had the honor of being promoted by a Marine, Brigadier General Flanagan. I was then selected to command an artillery battalion.

I had requested Fort Bragg, but my path would take me to Fort Hood in Texas for what was to be my final duty station. I became Deep Strike 6, commander of the Second Battalion, Twentieth Field Artillery Regiment (Multiple Launch Rocket System), Fourth Infantry Division. The battalion's strength was around 450 soldiers, and in Iraq, as Task Force 2-20, we grew by another hundred.

It was a great bunch of soldiers. I took command in 2002 on the sixth of June, the anniversary of D-Day, in the same division that took Utah Beach. In January 2003 we got our orders for Iraq, and we were ready and well trained. This assignment was the culmination of years of training that began the first day I donned the Army uniform as a young high school JROTC cadet. I'd been prepared for this very moment, but I would not be prepared for what would come afterward.

In August 2003 we received intelligence reports that a particular Iraqi policeman had been providing information to the enemy, leading to an increase in ambushes on our patrols. We needed to detain the policeman for questioning because we believed something was about to happen in the next couple of days. I felt a sense of urgency, because my utmost concern was for the safety of those under my command.

The policeman had been stonewalling our interrogators, and we needed results. So I made the decision to put additional pressure on him with a psychological intimidation tactic. I drew my pistol and threatened to kill him if he did not provide information.

We took him outside, where he was held over a sand-filled weapons-clearing barrel. After a count of five, I fired my Beretta 9-millimeter pistol over his head into the sand. He began talking. He cried out for Allah and provided several names of individuals who intended to do harm to me and my unit. Afterward, there were no further attacks on my unit while it was under my command.

I immediately reported the incident and subsequently submitted to an investigation and Article 32 hearing. During the hearing my defense attorney, Marine Lieutenant Colonel Neal Puckett, asked if I would do it all again. Without hesitation I responded, "If it is about the lives and safety of my men, I would walk through hell with a gasoline can."

Ultimately, as a result of the hearing, I received an Article 15, a nonjudicial punishment similar to a traffic ticket. I was fined five thousand dollars, given an honorable discharge, and retired with full rank and benefits.

If Buck West had still been alive, he would have been proud. I had lived up to the parting words he shared back in October 1983 as I prepared to depart for Fort Sill: "Most of all, take care of your men." I faced the test and lived up to the standard of all those who had been teachers, leaders, and mentors in my life. At the time I didn't realize the impact this event would have, how big it was perceived back in America, and how it truly changed my path.

I stood by my actions then, and I stand by them now.

Much has been written about the choice I made, and there have been plenty of jackasses who have called me a war criminal and worse.

What none of them realize is that everything in my life, especially my military life, had shaped me for the decision I made in that moment. Every mentor, every soldier whose eyes I had ever looked into, shaped me to make the stand that I did.

So as I continue in my life outside of the military, I know that I will continue to be a guardian not only of our republic but also of those men and women who have served, are serving, and shall serve. I will be relentless in defending those who have been willing to make the last full measure of devotion to their country. And for those who have indeed made that ultimate sacrifice, I shall guard their honor.

In closing this chapter, let me share these words of President Teddy Roosevelt, particularly for those who have never served this country and risked their lives to protect her:

> It is not the critic who counts; not the man who points out how the strong man stumbles, or where the doer of deeds could have done them better. The credit belongs to the man who is actually in the arena, whose face is marred by dust and sweat and blood; who strives valiantly; who errs, who comes short again and again, because there is no effort

without error and shortcoming; but who does actually strive to do the deeds; who knows great enthusiasms, the great devotions; who spends himself in a worthy cause; who at the best knows in the end the triumph of high achievement, and who at the worst, if he fails, at least fails while daring greatly, so that his place shall never be with those cold and timid souls who neither know victory nor defeat.

Chapter 3

MY WARRIOR'S CODE

✶ ✶ ✶ ✶ ✶ ✶ ✶ ✶ ✶ ✶ ✶ ✶

Tough, Proud, Disciplined.
—Colonel Denny R. Lewis, commander,
Eighteenth Field Artillery Brigade
(Airborne), 1997–1999

A t the US Army Command and General Staff College at Fort Leavenworth, it is the goal of every Army major to graduate from the school, move on to a duty station, and earn the prestigious positions of operations and executive officer at the battalion or brigade level. These are termed "branch qualifying" positions, and they're one of the primary ways of enhancing your chances to be selected for command of a battalion in your respective specialty. During this rite of passage, every major division would send its commanders or future commanders out for a recruiting visit. To put this into perspective, it was like the NFL combine, except you basically were being scouted, tried out, recruited, and drafted all at once.

In 1996 my desire for my next assignment was Fort Bragg. I'd come back from Korea and wanted to get back to an Airborne unit where I knew several incoming battalion commanders in the artillery.

Finally the moment arrived. Representatives from Fort Bragg and the XVIII Airborne Corps were up for their visit. Ahead of time I had learned that an incoming brigade commander named Denny Lewis was attending the Pre-Command Course.

Colonel Denny R. Lewis had an impeccable reputation, so I decided to write him an introductory letter and place it in his Pre-Command Course mailbox. As a result I was invited to a dinner with incoming Eighty-Second Airborne Division artillery commander Colonel Jay Hood, who had been my very first battery commander in Italy back in 1984, and with the incoming commander of the Eighteenth Field Artillery Brigade (Airborne), Colonel Lewis.

I'd never met Denny Lewis before, but doggone, was he one tough SOB. He was a martial arts expert at one time and had tried out for the elite Army counterterrorism unit, Delta Force. He was a quiet man and very discerning. That evening you could tell he was sizing up all of us, like a Roman consul general evaluating his potential line of field commanders. Colonel Lewis would ask simple questions, and it was clear he was carefully analyzing each word in the response. I certainly was nervous, but knew I couldn't show any trepidation among my peers because I realized we were in competition. That dinner in Leavenworth, Kansas, was the beginning of an incredible mentorship from a man who would come to guide my understanding of what it meant to be the consummate warrior and leader.

I have encountered a number of outstanding leaders in my military career: Needham, Rokus, McNeill, Abizaid, Lescynski, Gingrich, Sullivan, Bedard, Berndt, Nyland, Boykin, Mundy, Rodriguez, Morris, Smoots, Kryschtal, John, Herspring, Bailey, McDonald, Schneider, Fontenot, Flake, Moreno, Ellis, Cannon, Anderson, and Helmick, to mention a few. There were senior enlisted men, command sergeant majors, and men like Ballogg, Mike and Larry Taylor, Norris Hand, Henry Burns, and Bernardo Aquino who taught and mentored me to be an exceptional soldier's soldier. But none would have the influence on me as the man I would forever refer to as "Denny R."

After that dinner in Leavenworth, I waited with bated breath because I hadn't interviewed with any other units while I was at the staff college. I wanted to don the maroon beret of an American paratrooper again, and I would not consider anything else.

Finally the orders arrived: I was to be assigned to Fort Bragg, to the XVIII Airborne Corps Artillery and the Eighteenth Field Artillery Brigade. Damn, was I stoked.

The biggest surprise was to come. Colonel Denny R. Lewis, Mr. Airborne Artillery, had selected me to be his brigade operations officer. Let me explain what this meant and what an honor it was. The brigade/regimental OpsO position is a senior billet. It lines candidates up for future battalion command, as normally a brigade OpsO has been a battalion OpsO. It meant I would regularly interact directly with the battalion commanders in the brigade and, most important, would have to earn their trust and respect. I could not believe it—I had been given the chance, the opportunity, and the immense responsibility of being in charge of the operations of the Army's largest artillery unit.

As "Steel 3" I learned from "Steel 6," Colonel Lewis, how to be tough, proud, but disciplined. I thought I knew what leadership was, but Colonel Lewis crystallized it for me. Leadership came down to five fundamentals: courage, competence, commitment, conviction, and character. I learned from Steel 6 to be daring and that there were times when a leader has to make a stand, however lonely or unpopular.

My wife, Angela, will tell you that as OpsO I spent many a night in my office, sleeping on the couch, because I never wanted to be caught short in my duties. At age thirty-six, I was the youngest brigade-level operations officer at Fort Bragg, and I had to carry myself in a manner that clearly conveyed I'd earned the privilege.

I knew that some folks would be watching to see if I would fail. I had to display enough courage that no one would ever believe I felt unqualified or unprepared for this position.

Leadership skills were Colonel Lewis's foremost gifts to me. Beyond that, I was learning my craft from one of the most competent artillerymen I had ever known. When Colonel Lewis and I discussed training and deployment readiness, I was learning from a master, since he had been the Eighty-Second Airborne Division artillery operations officer and a phenomenal artillery battalion commander. I learned how to walk up to a firing position, evaluate the site, and ascertain the nuances of artillery preparedness before anyone opened their mouth.

I learned not just military operations but the art of decision making. Our brigade motto was "Sweat saves blood." That simple phrase showed me how a guiding principle can inspire excellence and a sense of compassion for your soldiers. A strong motto can set high standards and instill in your troops a sense of pride in achieving those standards.

Some people believe that to be compassionate you must lower standards to make a task or goal easier for everybody to achieve. But I learned from Colonel Lewis that such an approach makes a unit mediocre. "Sweat saves blood" declared that hard training—steel sharpening steel—guaranteed success, developed individual strength and pride, and promoted a level of superiority.

When one day Colonel Lewis said he wanted to create the ultimate military endurance competition, many thought he was nuts. But I understood exactly what Denny R. wanted. So when we held and competed in the first Fort Bragg Perimeter Challenge race, his unit knew what it meant to be a warrior, to truly be tough, proud, and disciplined.

With that one project, I learned Colonel Lewis had the courage to attempt something that had never been done before. He had the ability to deliver his vision easily, whereas others may have struggled to communicate their goals.

Working together we designed an endurance race that spanned the entire outer base perimeter, encompassing a ruck march (a long walk with a heavy backpack), lake crossing, land navigation, simulated casualty evacuation, and marathon run. Denny R. was absolutely committed to this event and knew it would be an opportunity to display the professionalism of the soldiers in his brigade and his commitment to toughness—something we need to resurrect not just in our military but in our American culture.

Of all the leadership skills I honed during this period, it was the last lesson that was most important to me—character. Colonel Lewis taught me that regardless of who was around, it was important to do what's right. And it was our corps artillery commanding general, Geoff Miller, who coined the phrase "Leaders know what right looks like." Character is simply defined as doing what is right when no one is watching.

Courage, competence, commitment, conviction, and character were the fundamental principles of leadership I learned from a man who, had he been born centuries before in Japan, truly would have been a samurai master—"Steel 6," Colonel Denny R. Lewis.

These principles form my personal warrior's code and combine with honor and integrity to shape my personality. I often wonder what Capitol Hill would look like if more elected officials possessed the same code. It would be a code that when violated would result in personal shame. Now, I'm not advocating politicians sit on the East Capitol steps and commit seppuku or ritual suicide (although some might welcome it). But I believe we've come to a point in America where our elected officials possess no code whatsoever. There is a lack of courage to be truthful with the American people and tell them what they *need* to hear, not just the words that some poll has confirmed will win election or reelection.

Let me make myself very clear. I did not enjoy losing a congressional election. But I did and will continue to make a stand, even if alone, to convey to my fellow Americans the truth and what they must hear.

The situation in which we find our country today is a direct result of a lack of competence. I will be the first to state I do not believe the best and brightest of America occupy elected positions, especially in Washington, DC, and, as of 2013, in our White House. Americans have devolved from demanding competent leadership to simply choosing another "American Idol," aided by a complicit media machine and an entertainment industry I wish would stick to playing make-believe and singing songs instead of attempting political punditry. We have lost our sense of commitment and conviction to our core values and principles, so that it seems the Declaration of Independence, the Federalist Papers, and the United States Constitution are viewed as relics to be crated and buried in some giant warehouse like the last scene in *Raiders of the Lost Ark.*

And when it comes to character, well, how many more despicable stories, broadcast simply to feed the twenty-four-hour news cycle, must we hide from our children? I know perfection is unattainable, but as a nation and a culture, we should at least desire to strive for it. I learned that one should never allow the perfect to be the enemy of the good enough, but today we don't even have good enough.

In the Army, indeed throughout the military, there are consequences to violating the code of leadership, our Bushido, or "way of the warrior." You will be relieved of command and not allowed further promotion.

Some would then say, "Well, LTC West, *you* were

relieved of command." Yes, I was, in the aftermath of the interrogation, but I stand by my decision and the action I took in Iraq. Why? Because the man I most highly respected, the personification of a warrior, Colonel Denny R. Lewis, stood by my decision as well. He got in contact with me in Iraq. He told me he was pissed off about the way I was being treated and called the action taken by my division commander pure unadulterated BS. In fact, it was ol' Denny R. who leaked the story to *Washington Times* writer Rowan Scarborough and gave it national exposure.

I always kept in mind that the motto of the Second Battalion, Twentieth Field Artillery Regiment (Multiple Launch Rocket System), which I commanded, was "Duty not reward." It was a motto that meant selfless service, self-sacrifice, commitment to duty—and it implied that my duty was first and foremost to the men I had been selected to command.

At the most critical point in my military career, God had presented me with the ultimate test and challenge of the principles in which I said I believed. I was to take steady fire from personal attacks and misinformation that continues still today, but I was ready. I knew what it meant to be a warrior. I knew what it meant to make a courageous stand. I knew this was the test that would set me on a different path than what I thought life had in store for me.

My life now has taken a new turn, yet my core values have not changed: service to God, country, and family. I have had many earthly masters who have been instrumental in developing me as an American ronin. Often, when I am traveling, complete strangers come up to me and thank me for being who I am. And who am I?

Just a simple servant, a regular fella who, for whatever reason, finds himself in this incredible position. I've never been comfortable being in the limelight or on the grand stage, and I never wanted to come off like some cheap, fake actor.

The underlying theme for me is to restore this republic. We must recommit to our fundamental principles and values. We must reclaim our American pride and exceptionalism. For that to happen, we must distance ourselves from a political class of elites and their accomplices in the media and entertainment industry who defile our culture and promote the degradation of honor and integrity.

Armed with the code of Bushido, the American ronin who will serve the people must arise. Americans must find leaders who possess the qualities of our Founding Fathers, not these present shameful usurpers and impostors.

Now is that time. The fakes, phonies, and frauds know it, which is why the courageous, competent, and committed true leaders for the next generation of America are viciously attacked and maligned.

I am not the only person who lives according to the motto of that storied American unit, the Thirty-Fourth Armored Regiment: "Fear God, and dread not." The code that brought me to this point in life is rooted in the words of God to Joshua in Deuteronomy 31:6: "Be strong and courageous for the Lord thy God shall never leave you nor forsake you."

It is that courage that our ancestors found to create this great nation and from which it has become an incredible land of opportunity in 237 short years. It is this nation, the greatest the world has ever known, that has provided me—and anyone who dares accept the challenge—with the chance to be more than they can be and to rise like a phoenix in her service. It is America that has instilled in me a burning desire to ensure that her greatest days lie ahead.

There are those who say I am extreme, too combative, or too "in your face," but it is the only way I know.

Colonel Lewis commanded the Fifth Battalion, Eighth Field Artillery Regiment and fought to have the unit designated Air Assault. He then began the process of having the unit redesignated as the First Battalion (Air Assault), 377th Field Artillery Regiment, to reconnect the unit to its history as a glider artillery outfit in World War II and to its service at Normandy.

After serving as his brigade operations officer for a year, Colonel Lewis assigned me to be the executive officer in the unit he had created, where our salute and challenge was "Be bold, Air Assault." Since that day, the ultimate code of this warrior has been, and will forever be: "Be bold."

"Fortune favors the bold," said Alexander the Great. So far, in my life, his words have been right on target.

PART II

CONSERVATIVE PRINCIPLES

Chapter 4

PHILOSOPHICAL FOUNDATIONS

★ ★ ★ ★ ★ ★ ★ ★ ★ ★ ★ ★

*And for the support of this Declaration,
with a firm reliance on the protection of
divine Providence, we mutually pledge to
each other our Lives, our Fortunes, and our
sacred Honor.*

—THOMAS JEFFERSON

These are the closing words of the Declaration of Independence, the document that inaugurated the American experiment in freedom. The story of the founding of our nation—and the men who risked everything to bring it about—is an amazing one.

Sadly, it is a story we seldom retell our children and grandchildren. As a result, when future generations make decisions for the future of this nation, they will be dangerously ill-informed. Lacking an understanding of the philosophical foundation of our republic, they may be more inclined to vote for its transformation into something our founders wouldn't recognize.

I started college thinking I would be an engineer just like my Uncle Jerome, who had graduated from Tennessee State University and worked for NASA. But I soon realized that although I enjoyed math, I didn't have the mind for engineering. I was passionate about logic and reason, but I discovered that my true talent lay in analyzing theories of history and political institutions, not mathematical theorems. I changed my major to political science, and I was immediately enthralled. I eventually earned two master's degrees: one from Kansas State University in political science and the second from the US Army Command and General Staff College in military arts and sciences. I developed my own philosophical foundation and acquired a deeper understanding of the political ideologies and theories that shape the world.

As I pursued my philosophical development, I began to wonder who had inspired our Founding Fathers when they created our nation. What led them to write such monumental documents as the Declaration of Independence, the Constitution of the United States, and the Federalist Papers?

Now, I know some folks might find this subject a bit dry. After all, I spent a bit of time teaching history to high school students, and it was tough to get them fired up—and most adults today are worse, preferring the steady diet of easy-to-digest sound bites they're fed by the media.

But the way I see it, nothing is more stimulating than understanding the DNA of our exceptional nation. What motivated these men to risk their lives and fortunes for generations they would never know? We're all beneficiaries of the legacy our founders left, so I think we owe them a little time to consider their roots.

Rather than try to get inside the heads of Jefferson, Madison, Jay, and Hamilton, I'd like to share my understanding of their inspiration and the principles that led them to create these great United States of America. And if a simple fella from the inner city of Atlanta can understand this, then just about anyone else probably can, too.

One of the fundamental premises that enabled our Founding Fathers to establish America was the theory of a "social contract," the notion that the ruler and those over whom he ruled agreed upon their respective roles and obligations. Of course in history there have been many differing perspectives on those roles, but the underlying implication was that the ruler governed by the consent of the governed. This concept was firmly delineated in the Declaration of Independence: "That to secure these rights, Governments are instituted among Men, deriving their just powers from the consent of the governed, that whenever any Form of Government becomes destructive of these ends, it is the Right of the People to alter or to abolish it, and to institute new Government. . . ."

Jefferson codified the social contract theory and sent a clear, brilliantly stated message that violation of the contract by any form of government would lose the consent of the governed, giving the governed the right to alter or abolish the relationship.

The social contract theory was rooted in the concept of popular sovereignty, which claimed that the ultimate source of legitimacy and authority for the state is the people. A social contract combined with popular sovereignty resulted in the belief that the state—in other words, government—was and is created by the individuals within it.

We must never forget that our country was established with preeminent regard for the individual—not the ruler, not the president, not the politburo, not a bunch of czars, but the individual.

Balancing the rights of the individual against those of society has always been a struggle. It has also been a constant ideological tussle to define the relationship between the individual and the government. Three very different men shaped how we would regard that relationship in America: Thomas Hobbes, John Locke, and Jean-Jacques Rousseau.

Fundamentally, Hobbes, Locke, and Rousseau shared the basic belief that people had once existed without government but had been governed by natural law in a predetermined state of nature. The three men concurred that people were basically equal under natural law and that political power derived from the individual. However, their respective definitions of "freedom" differed in important ways.

For Hobbes, freedom was possible only when the individuals in society subjected themselves to the monarch. Locke believed freedom was greatest when the individual was left alone. Rousseau saw human freedom as attainable only with the creation of an ordered society in which equality was a dominant principle.

In this regard Hobbes and Rousseau were closely aligned, because for them freedom was subordinate to a sovereign authority. Locke favored a more parliamentary republic in which government arbitrated disputes among citizens. He also advocated for private property but was against unlimited accumulation. Rousseau, because of his focus on universal equality, opposed unequal distribution of property because it resulted in unequal political influence.

To understand how and why each of these gentlemen came to their respective points of view, it's useful to review their historical contexts.

From 1646 to 1648, Thomas Hobbes was a math tutor for the young Prince of Wales (later King Charles II), then exiled in Paris during the English Civil War. The war was between those backing an unpopular King Charles I (Charles II's father) and the Parliamentarians, led by Oliver Cromwell (as I learned as a young boy by watching the movie *Cromwell* with Richard Harris in the title role). Amazingly, with the defeat of forces loyal to Charles I and his subsequent execution in 1649, power wasn't transferred to his son and heir Charles II but to the people. For the next eleven years, England was ruled by Cromwell and the Parliamentarians. But after the death of Cromwell and the collapse of his regime, the newly formed Convention Parliament declared Charles II rightful king of England, and he triumphantly ascended the throne on his thirtieth birthday.

It's no surprise that Hobbes, after witnessing such turmoil, considered monarchy the best form of government. His view of the common man was certainly not pretty. He believed that in a state of nature where people were free to act as they wished with no law to govern them, they would lose all civility, if not humanity. In his book *Leviathan*, Hobbes used rather politically incorrect terms to describe the hopeless, chaotic, and "hideous, violent, brutish, nasty" state in which man existed. Hobbes felt we were all prisoners of our own avarice, although deep down we maintained a sense of rational thought. "Freedom," though certainly not in the sense we think of it today, was possible only if people surrendered their liberty to a monarch. Being naturally wicked (not to mention hideous, violent, brutish, and nasty), the common man could only experience freedom when restrained and checked by a superior authority.

Needless to say, Hobbes served Charles II, his young master, well. But his view would not be entirely accepted by our Constitutional Framers, though it was instrumental in their understanding of governing systems.

Charles II had no legitimate heirs but fathered many children, of whom he acknowledged "only" fourteen. On his death his brother, James II, succeeded him to the throne.

The reign of King James II was stormy. He took Hobbesian theory to heart and sought absolute power. As he increased his ties to the Roman Catholic Church, he used his power to suppress any rebellion from his former allies, the Protestant members of Parliament. His policies of religious intolerance finally came to a head when he was overthrown during the Glorious Revolution by the English Parliamentarians, with assistance from his own daughter's husband, William of Orange. In 1688 James II fled to France, closing a long struggle between king and Parliament for dominance.

Before the ascent of a new monarch, Parliament adopted a bill of rights designed to enforce strict limits on the English monarchy. The English Bill of Rights gave Parliament the right to hold free elections, meet frequently, legislate, and petition the king. In turn, the king was not allowed to suspend an act of Parliament and was forbidden to tax or to keep a standing army in peacetime without Parliament's approval.

Against this backdrop John Locke gained prominence. From exile in Holland, he returned to England escorting Mary, Princess of Orange, who later became queen beside William of Orange after the Glorious Revolution. As Hobbes sought to validate the restoration of the Stuart dynasty, Locke sought to promote the Glorious Revolution and its result.

Today Locke is regarded as the preeminent classical liberal. Locke, too, was an advocate of "natural law," but his interpretation of the term offered certain rights to the individual that could not be legally taken away or alienated without due process. Those rights were defined by Locke as life, liberty, and estate (property). Locke was most specific about the individual's right to private property, which he believed was essential to each person's well-being. That said, Locke did not embrace unchecked accumulation of property, and he favored a free market as being most conducive to individual freedom while preventing great disparities in property ownership.

Locke's fundamental premise was that private property was not created by society, and therefore society had no special claim or control over it. Private property was created by private individuals. I guess Locke believed "You *did* build that."

While Hobbes promoted freedom as being granted and possible only under government, Locke took a completely different approach. Locke maintained that people were most free when unhindered by government. Locke stated that freedom existed only in the absence of restraint, because, as rational people, we would of course behave decently when left alone. We could exercise our rights without the yoke of regulation as long as we chose not to interfere with the rights of others.

Individual equality was another aspect of natural law. Locke recognized that all individuals differed widely in mental and physical capacity, but he asserted that regardless of these obvious differences, all individuals have the same natural rights. Locke also said that individuals were united by common interests, but that any government should function solely as an agent of the society, strictly limited to providing its vital function of serving the people. Finally, Locke was a proponent of majority rule, with a parliament elected by property owners. He called for separation of the executive (royal) and legislative (parliamentary) powers, with the legislature, as the direct agent of the people, having precedence over the executive. The legislature created the policy, while the executive carried it out.

By the time of Locke's death in 1704, the "Age of Enlightenment" had spread across Europe, challenging ideas grounded in tradition and faith and promoting scientific thought, the elimination of religious and monarchical authority from the education and legislative process, and the advancement of democracy.

It was also the coming of age for an itinerant musician, music copyist, teacher, and composer named Jean-Jacques Rousseau. Born in Geneva in 1712, Rousseau had a challenging childhood. His mother died nine days after his birth. When Jean-Jacques was ten, his father abandoned him to avoid imprisonment for fighting in a duel, and the young Rousseau was raised by his mother's relatives. Rousseau left home at age sixteen and spent many years wandering and having adventures. He traveled to Italy to study the Roman Catholic faith, then headed to France to the home (and bed) of an older woman, and eventually landed in Paris. He married his mistress, an illiterate servant who bore him five children, all of whom were abandoned at birth to the foundling hospital. It was not until 1749, when he was thirty-seven, that Rousseau made his mark, winning an essay contest sponsored by the Academy of Dijon with his essay, now known as his *First Discourse,* describing how society had corrupted human nature.

Rousseau is often referred to as the founder of modern radical thought. Primarily, what separated Rousseau from Locke was his perspective on private property. Rousseau held that private property developed only after a community was formed, but it always promoted greed and selfishness. He believed people should form a new society to which they would surrender themselves completely. But in contrast to Hobbes's assertion that a benevolent monarchy should lead, in Rousseau's vision this new society would become a "public person" as a whole, directed by the "general will." If created by the majority in the interest of the greater society, the general will could not be wrong. As a result, anyone who refused to comply with the general will, and by extension their own interests as determined by the new society, would be forced to comply. According to Rousseau, when the community controls the state, it creates moral authority itself, thereby joining moral authority and state within a secular setting.

The lesson to be gleaned from comparing Hobbes and Rousseau is that two similar ideas can result in two different extremes. Hobbes promoted subjugation of the people to a singular monarch, while Rousseau advocated subjugation of the people to a secular general will. But neither Hobbes nor Rousseau recognized the preeminence of the individual.

A final and important piece of our governing structure came from two other gentlemen of the Age of Enlightenment. While less well known than Locke and Rousseau, James Harrington and Charles-Louis de Secondat Montesquieu were still influential, and it was from Montesquieu that James Madison derived the theory of separation of powers, and of checks and balances. Both Harrington and Montesquieu were attracted to the idea of a democratic republic that limited the power of government over the people. This concept helped inspire Madison to create three branches of government, with respective duties, responsibilities, and powers not concentrated in any one branch.

Madison went one step further and developed the theory of federalism to separate powers between the levels of government: federal and state. Madison sought to preclude any level of government from gaining too much power. And of course, inspired by the English Bill of Rights, the United States' first ten Amendments to the Constitution codified the preeminence and specific rights of individuals as well as the rights and powers of the state.

Hobbes, Locke, and Rousseau had three very different governing philosophies, which are still being argued to this very day. What amazes me is that Locke, the father of classical liberalism, would almost certainly be viewed as a conservative today. I recall speaking to a political science class at Florida Atlantic University and expressing in my opening remarks that today's modern conservatism is most closely aligned with classical liberalism, with its theories of individual sovereignty, limited government, and inalienable rights of life, liberty, and property. Well, the students went apoplectic, shouting their derision, until I turned to the professor and asked the simple question, "Am I correct, sir?" To the students' dismay, the answer was yes.

This is one of my biggest frustrations and concerns about America. Our electorate doesn't have a freaking clue about who we are or from whence we came. Too many voters seem to be mindless lemmings who fall prey to droning gimmicks and slogans like "Hope and Change" or "Forward." Even more disturbing is a media industry and "intellectual" elite who are complicit in not taking to task or challenging the empty, rhetorical, poll-tested crap being fed to our country.

If you have a son or daughter who is a senior in high school, ask him or her to define natural law and popular sovereignty. Ask your child who Thomas Hobbes, John Locke, and Jean-Jacques Rousseau are. But first see if you can answer those questions yourself.

Earlier I mentioned watching the movie *Cromwell* as a boy. It was because I had parents who forced me to read and learn beyond the education I was receiving that I grew to appreciate not only history but my own country. They inspired in me an inquisitiveness I maintain today.

John Locke, the classical liberal Englishman, gave our Founding Fathers a blueprint to create the world's longest-running constitutional republic. Locke also gave us the governing philosophy we now call conservatism. I find it kinda funny that these folks who today call themselves liberals really have no clue what they are and what they represent. Unfortunately, those in power do. These liberal elites do not represent the governing philosophy of classical liberalism but rather the postmodern kind, which seeks not to increase the power of the individual but the power of the state.

But I'm getting a little ahead of myself. First I want to share the modern conservative governing principles for which I so proudly stand guard.

Chapter 5

GOVERNING PRINCIPLES

* * * * * * * * * * * * * *

The Constitution is not an instrument for
the government to restrain the people, it is
an instrument for the people to restrain the
government.

—Patrick Henry

History, in general, only informs us what bad
government is. Most bad government has
grown out of too much government.

—Thomas Jefferson

If men were angels, no government would
be necessary. If angels were to govern men,
neither external nor internal controls on
government would be necessary.

—James Madison, *The Federalist Papers*

America stands today as the longest-running constitutional republic. It is surely one of humanity's greatest political feats that an insignificant collection of thirteen colonies could band together, fight a revolution against the greatest power in the world, and create a government—all at the same time.

Our Founding Fathers were incredibly learned. They understood profoundly the complexity of their task. From the words of Thomas Jefferson in the Declaration of Independence to the brilliance of James Madison in the Constitution and the Federalist Papers, they created something that had previously existed only in theories and dreams.

Is America a perfect place? Well, of course we can't ever hope to be perfect, but our founders wanted us to be the best and greatest provider of opportunity to those who have and will set foot upon our shores (preferably legally).

At the time of our nation's creation, even its citizens had trouble wrapping their minds around this new concept of governance. According to accounts of the day, the founders and deputies chosen for the Constitutional Convention of 1787 worked behind closed doors. Anxious citizens gathered outside, waiting for results. As the doors opened and the delegates emerged, a Mrs. Powell of Philadelphia stopped Benjamin Franklin and asked him point-blank, "Well, Doctor, what have we got, a republic or a monarchy?" Without hesitation he responded, "A republic, madam, if you can keep it." Even at the time of its founding, our nation's creators realized the difficulty of maintaining freedom, liberty, and checks and balances when doing so depended solely on the will of the people.

Thomas Jefferson looked into the future when he said, "Freedom is lost gradually from an uninterested, uninformed, and uninvolved people." I wonder if he also foresaw reality TV shows? Sadly, his prediction is coming true. A quickly expanding portion of our electorate has no understanding of—and worse, no interest in learning about—the philosophical foundations and governing principles of its own nation.

While Jefferson and the framers of the Constitution could only guess what would happen in the future to their new republic, there can be no doubt they had learned the lessons of the past. From their more contemporary European political philosophers to those of ancient Greece and Rome, our founders recognized there had to be a careful balance of power and a fundamental belief in the rights of the individual for their bold experiment to succeed.

So what were the governing principles the founders established for America? I believe there were six: limited government, fiscal responsibility, a free market, individual sovereignty, a strong national defense, and an understanding that all of man's freedoms come ultimately from God.

When they created this nation, limited government was at the top of the founders' list. In the forty-sixth of eighty-five essays known now as the Federalist Papers, it was James Madison who wrote: "the ambitious encroachments of the federal government, on the authority of the state governments, would not excite the opposition of a single state, or of a few states only. They would be signals of general alarm." Today in America we are witnessing the encroachment of the federal government into nearly every aspect of our lives. Amazingly, people seem to have become almost immune to this encroachment, as long as they can maintain a tolerable existence. Sometimes I feel like I'm in the movie *The Matrix,* where there were two worlds: the real world, where I live, and a virtual world, where many Americans prefer to exist because they are free to indulge every pleasure—even at the cost of their own free will.

In June 1788, when 168 Virginia delegates met to ratify or reject the Constitution, James Madison warned that liberty could quietly slip away as "abridgment of the freedom of the people by gradual and silent encroachments were more frequent by those in power than by violent and sudden usurpations."

Being from the South, I always like to make an analogy between encroaching government and boiling a frog. You never want to toss the frog into a pot of boiling water. Instead, you plop the happy little frog in a pot of cold water and slowly but surely turn up the heat. It is no different with today's expansive growth of government into our daily lives.

While you're waiting for the water to boil, you might take a quick read of the entire Declaration of Independence to get a sense of the encroachment Jefferson experienced "under a long train of abuses and usurpations."

The purpose of the Declaration of Independence was to lay out the grievances of the thirteen colonies against an intrusive and invasive monarchical government. The list of twenty-seven grievances described by Jefferson and signed by fifty-six patriots formed the foundation for the republic's guiding principle of limited government.

In his book *The Founders' Key,* Hillsdale College President Dr. Larry Arnn eloquently presented the relationship between the Declaration and the Constitution:

> *The arrangements of the Constitution have a way of organizing our actions so as to produce certain desirable results, and they have done this more reliably than any governing instrument in the history of man. Connect these arrangements to the beauty of the Declaration and one has something inspiring and commanding.*

Our country is now at risk of forgetting the value of limited government. We are told bigger government is necessary for the general welfare of our citizens. Instead of sticking to its primary constitutional tasks of promoting the general welfare and providing for the common defense, we have a government that is focused on *providing* welfare, and who cares about defense? As the temperature in the pot heats up, we have gradually moved from securing the endorsed inalienable rights of life, liberty, and the pursuit of happiness to demanding a "guarantee of happiness." But to guarantee happiness, the government's powers must be unlimited.

If government's power is unlimited, its spending will most likely be as well, for how better to retain power? In 1850 the French economist and classic liberal theorist Frédéric Bastiat predicted what we would be living through 160 years later in his essay "The Law": "When plunder becomes a way of life for a group of men living together in society, they create for themselves in the course of time a legal system that authorizes it and a moral code that glorifies it."

Politicians know exactly what they need to do to get reelected, and building and maintaining big government has become a huge business.

In Ayn Rand's novel *Atlas Shrugged,* the dashing Latin copper magnate Francisco d'Anconia delivered a warning we should heed today:

When you see that trading is done, not by consent, but by compulsion—when you see that in order to produce, you need to obtain permission from men who produce nothing—when you see that money is flowing to those who deal not in goods, but in favors—when you see that men get richer by graft and by pull than by work, and your laws don't protect you against them, but protect them against you—when you see corruption being rewarded and honesty becoming a self-sacrifice—you may know that your society is doomed.

Can it be our grand experiment in liberty, freedom, and democracy has run its course? Can it be we have reached a tipping point from which there is no possible return? Are we looking into the abyss with one foot dangling over the edge? I certainly hope not. But we would be wise to heed the warnings. By the mid-1800s, French historian Alexis de Tocqueville already knew what dire fate might await us:

A democracy cannot exist as a permanent form of government. It can only exist until the voters discover that they can vote themselves largesse from the public treasury. From that moment on, the majority always votes for the candidates promising the most benefits from the public treasury with the result

*being that a democracy always collapses over loose
fiscal policy, always followed by a dictatorship.*

Our nation now has a massive debt of seventeen *trillion* dollars. If the government were to set aside one dollar per second, it would take 31,688 years to pay off just one trillion, and 507,008 years to pay off the other sixteen—not including the interest on the debt. But you and every other taxpayer in this nation for generations to come are on the hook for all of it. The only way the government can pay off the debt or spend more is to take more from you. And it doesn't seem to me that government's voracious appetite will slow down anytime soon.

The idea that governments, not the free market, could stimulate demand and growth was chiefly promoted in the 1930s by John Maynard Keynes, a British economist and early progressive. In fact Keynes was also a proponent of eugenics, which advocates improving human hereditary traits by promoting higher reproduction among more desired people and reduced reproduction from those deemed less so—an idea shared by a certain infamous figure in Germany.

Nonetheless Keynes's theories were widely adopted by Western economies from the 1940s through the 1960s, until they began to fail in the 1970s. No economy has ever thrived when governments continually raise taxes to spend money they don't have. Alexander Hamilton, our first secretary of the treasury, knew exactly why this could never work in a free society: "If congress can employ money indefinitely to the general welfare ... the powers of congress would subvert the very foundation, the very nature of the limited government established by the people of America." I only wish our recent and current treasury secretaries held the same belief.

Obviously our Founding Fathers recognized that an invasive and intrusive government would need ever more revenue through ever more onerous taxation to feed its exponential growth, which is why fiscal responsibility was number two on their list of governing principles.

Today, under the guise of so-called benevolence, terms like *shared sacrifice, fairness, fair share,* and *economic patriotism* are used to justify higher taxes. Such terms guilt the citizenry into accepting the system of legal plunder.

But even plunder runs out eventually, and those being plundered tend not to agree to it willingly. As Jefferson understood, "The democracy will cease to exist when you take away from those who are willing to work and give to those who would not."

Jefferson also believed that "to compel a man to furnish funds for the propagation of ideas he disbelieves and abhors is sinful and tyrannical." I am quite certain our founders would abhor the immense national debt accrued since January 2009 when the Obama administration shifted spending into high gear. Jefferson warned us to "place economy among the first and most important republican virtues, and public debt as the greatest of the dangers to be feared." Maybe at the next Democrat-hosted Jefferson-Jackson dinner, they'll read that quote. After all, it comes from the person they're supposedly celebrating.

If a government is truly limited in its scope, it naturally operates within its constitutionally prescribed duties and responsibilities. However, when government extends its mandates under the guise of "benevolence" but in practice doles out rewards for electoral allegiance, it becomes fiscally irresponsible.

We continually hear the emotional argument about government providing a safety net for those who have fallen on hard times or who have no means of support. There is no doubt that as a nation we should take care of those who have fallen off the ladder of opportunity. But the problem is, the safety net gradually becomes a hammock.

There's nothing new about this problem. Benjamin Franklin recognized it when he offered his own solution: "I am for doing good to the poor, but I differ in opinion of the means. I think the best way of doing such good to the poor, is not making them easy in poverty, but leading or driving them out of it."

Measured against our fundamental governing principles, we clearly do not have good government—heck, we suck! We have excessive debt, growing poverty, exploding deficits, an expanding nanny state, and an anemic economy. The sad thing is, there seems to be no reprieve in sight. Why? Because, as a nation, we have become uninterested, uninformed, and disengaged from the truth. In these almost Orwellian times, when the government routinely makes up doublespeak phrases like "man-caused disasters," and government officials regularly lie about everything from their personal lives to the cost of government-run health care, telling the truth becomes a revolutionary act. I'm not sure anyone would accuse me of starting a revolution, but I know from experience that telling the truth doesn't always win friends.

Regarding the third governing principle of a free market, our nation was founded on the belief in a higher authority, that we all have the right to pursue happiness by our own will, limited only by our own determination to produce. And as we produce for ourselves, we create greater opportunities for others as well. But when this free marketplace of ideas and personal enterprise is made subject to the power of those in government, the economy withers, and so do freedom and liberty. In the words of James Madison in essay fourteen of the Federalist Papers: "As a man is said to have a right to his property, he may be equally said to have a property in his rights."

The most dangerous result of government's stranglehold on the free market is the slow and steady erosion of our country's most important resource: the individual. Madison knew the rights of the individual needed to be paramount, for "the rights of persons, and the rights of property, are the objects for the protection of which Government was instituted."

Our founders realized that government had to be limited, for if it was limited, it would more likely be fiscally responsible. And if it was fiscally responsible, it could not usurp the capital and therefore the individual sovereignty of its citizens.

This fourth fundamental governing principle of individual sovereignty was as essential as the first two in ensuring the existence of the nation. According to our founders, the government should never seek to subjugate the individual to the state—quite the opposite. We must never forget that our Constitution was not deemed complete until it included a Bill of Rights.

We are currently experiencing an onslaught against one of our constitutional rights, the Second Amendment, which guarantees the right of the people to keep and bear arms. When the coauthor of this amendment, George Mason, was asked what he meant by a "militia," he replied, "It is the whole people. To disarm the people is the best and most effectual way to enslave them." Our founders realized an armed American is a citizen, but an unarmed American is a subject. They wrote the Second Amendment to ensure we never lost our rights to the first—or our rights to freedom itself. Mason's fellow Virginian Thomas Jefferson made clear that "The strongest reason for the people to retain their right to keep

With my mom and little brother Arlan (center) around 1972 in a family picture taken at Mom's work, the Sixth US Marine Corps District Headquarters in Atlanta. Dad was never one for staged portraits, plus he was probably sleeping since he worked the night shift at the Veterans Administration Hospital. Whenever I visited Mom at her office, I knew to be respectful and address Marines and the civilians as "Sir" and "Ma'am." I hoped one day I'd be like those men and women in uniform. (West family photo)

With Mom and Dad on Commissioning Day, July 31, 1982, at the University of Tennessee Army ROTC Office in Stokely Athletic Center. I'd just returned from ROTC Advanced Camp in Fort Lewis, Washington, and still had a year of school to complete. But because of my experience in high school ROTC, I advanced faster in the college program. You can see that Buck West smirk, but I knew inside Dad was beaming. After all those years at the Sixth Marine Corps District, Mom finally got to pin the bars on her own officer. (West family photo)

Me as a second lieutenant, Delta Battery, Fourth Battalion, 325th Airborne Battalion Combat Team (ABCT), Vicenza, Italy, 1984. Before there was a Third Ranger Battalion, there was the ABCT in Vicenza, Italy. Our unit was deployed nine months out of the year to various locations related to our contingency missions. During this assignment, I learned to ski, but the most memorable moment was when I passed through Checkpoint Charlie into East Berlin. It was in East Berlin that I saw what communism/socialism was all about. (West family photo)

Colonel Denny R. Lewis, commander of the Eighteenth Field Artillery Brigade (Airborne), 1997–1999. To look into his eyes is to understand our brigade motto, "Sweat Saves Blood." Colonel Lewis taught me to have a commander's vision and to understand operational planning and execution. He gave me an unheard-of opportunity, allowing a fresh-out-of-Staff-College major to be the operations officer of the largest Field Artillery unit in the US Army. Denny Lewis is now chairman of the Allen West Guardian Fund, which supports military and minority conservative candidates for federal elected office. He is a true patriot. *(US Army official portrait)*

With Corporal Robert Delgado in Kuwait, March 2003. Del was from Texas, a stellar young soldier, and an excellent driver with a meticulous attention to detail. I'll never forget the night he was shot. We were heading to the rally point for a major raid operation against an insurgent weapons cache when we were suddenly hit by a vehicle drive-by ambush. Del was hit in the chest, but the bullet ricocheted off and went into his arm. We eliminated the enemy, and as I knelt down over Del he said, "Sir, the mutha!@#$er shot me." I responded, "We shot them back." He testified at the Article 32 hearing, and we remain close to this day. *(West family photo)*

With Pastor Jim Vineyard at the Windsor Hill Baptist Church in Oklahoma City, summer 2004. Pastor Vineyard knew the story from Iraq and wanted to have me out for a dinner and awards recognition ceremony. A funny note: This church was an Evangelical Christian one where typical female attire was long dresses, but my wife, Angela, showed up dressed like a "South Florida chick." I'll never forget Angela and the girls heading over to a Walmart to change their attire—we believe in being respectful. Ultimately, we all had a great time. (*West family photo*)

This is how I roll, with my 2005 Honda VTX-1800N, which sports a custom US flag paint job by Chopper Zoo, Fort Lauderdale. The first motorcycle I rode was a Honda CBR 750 café racer when I was in Italy in 1985, but today I love my powerful VTX-1800 with the shaft drive and after-market pipes. Of course, I know some are saying, "Why ain't the Colonel on a Harley-Davidson?" Because I like my bike's uniqueness, I'm a fiscal conservative, and this bike happens to be very well priced. And as long as I put my American butt on it, it's American. (*Boris Balaban*)

Dishing out Five Guys at a grand opening in Fort Lauderdale off Cypress Creek Road, near our congressional district office in 2011. I love Five Guys and eat their food at least once a week. Serving on the House Small Business Committee made me look differently at franchisers like the family who owned the Five Guys. I wanted to understand the effects tax policy, regulations, and health-care mandates have on the entrepreneurs who are the backbone of our country. Too often, politicians come up with schemes to win over the electorate but never consider the second- and third-order effects. After I ended my tour of duty at the Five Guys, I treated myself to a nice cheeseburger. *(Boris Balaban)*

Surfacing after a reef cleanup dive off the shores of Lauderdale-by-the-Sea. We went out to clean and clear the fishing line that endangers the pristine reef system here in South Florida. Some say that conservatives don't care for the environment, but that's BS. I'd be happy to take anyone on a reef cleanup dive, and I want to see us secure more vessels to sink for artificial reefs. My initial SCUBA certification came when I was an ROTC cadet at Tennessee. I re-certified when I retired in 2004 and have achieved the level of Master SCUBA diver. *(Boris Balaban)*

Election night at the Boca Raton Marriott Hotel. A little-known fact about that night was that I didn't show up at the hotel until around 8:30 p.m. or so. I'd told very few people, besides Angela, that I'd be at our church with my pastor, Scott Eynon. We prayed for a while and then turned the results over to God. After that, we watched the classic film *The Robe*. Pastor Scott had never seen the film, so I gave him the movie to share with his family, then drove up the Sawgrass Expressway to Boca Raton. Those who didn't know where I was gave a sigh of relief. *(Palm Beach Post/ZUMApress.com)*

Swearing-in day, January 2011. From left: brother-in-law Roger Graham, cousin Anthony Wilson, Speaker John Boehner, niece Chiquitta, wife Angela, nephew Captain Bernard West, daughter Austen, daughter Aubrey (hidden), myself, and sister-in-law Jannetta. I was born in February 1961, and later that same year there was an event called the "wade-in" on Fort Lauderdale beach to protest segregation. Amazingly enough, fifty years later I was sworn in as the congressional representative of Fort Lauderdale beach. It was a day that my girls will always remember, and I know my parents were looking down on us with a smile. *(US House of Representatives)*

I had a great office and fantastic congressional staff. We were in the Longworth building, seventh floor, and I could look out onto the Library of Congress and the Supreme Court. Next door to me was Maryland congressman Chris Van Hollen. Sometimes I'd walk by his office and hear visitors say in tones usually reserved for the boogeyman, "That's Allen West." The best part of serving in that office was when families would come to visit, and I'd put the kids in the chair for pictures. Their faces would just light up. *(Boris Balaban)*

Lights, cameras, media . . . the aftermath of a town hall meeting in Deerfield Beach. Our standard operating procedure was to hold two town halls each month, one in Broward County and one in Palm Beach County. It was my responsibility to report back to our constituents every month at an open venue. No one could ever say that I hid from the people or that I lied. I'm not in Congress anymore, but these days I can look in the mirror and feel that I did my best. *(Mort Kuff)*

In September 2012 the "Romney for President" bus pulled into Traditions in Port St. Lucie, Florida. I was asked to give introductory comments before those of Florida attorney general Pam Bondi. The best part of the day was when my wife, daughters, and exchange student daughter met Ann Romney. I believe America regrets not having elected Governor Romney to the presidency. He and Mrs. Romney would have restored a sense of exceptionalism to America and a sense of honor to the office. Governor Romney certainly would have done better in restoring our economy. The reelection of President Obama was the ultimate mistake. *(Boris Balaban)*

CPAC 2013. I delivered the opening address, welcoming the audience to the fortieth CPAC. I remember my first CPAC, 2008. I'd just returned from Afghanistan and was running for Congress. I was a complete unknown and was just trying to hand out my card and meet as many people as I could. From a TV screen outside, I watched the proceedings and wondered what it would be like to speak on the grand stage. In 2010, I was invited to speak at CPAC, and it was phenomenal. In 2011, I was sitting at my favorite Chinese food place in Washington, DC, with my chief of staff, and he received a call asking me to be the CPAC keynote speaker. It was Tuesday and the speech was to be on Saturday, and without hesitation I said, "Yep!" I'd gone from handing out cards in 2008 to being a keynoter. America is awesome! *(Eric Draper)*

C'mon, man, I was Artillery—I never carried a machine gun! There were countless cartoon caricatures of me, some funny, others offensive. It's always humorous when progressives think they can "hurt my feelings." Do they fail to realize that I served in the Army for twenty-two years and have been in combat? Did you see that stare from Colonel Lewis? If anything, all this just made me relish the fact that I was getting under *their* skin. Am I a tough guy? Sure. But there are many who are far tougher, and I had the honor to serve with them. Vladimir Putin would never intimidate me or punk me out as he did our president. Furthermore, if I ever sit across the table from despots and dictators, I want this image in their heads. But next time, please give me a simple M4 carbine. *(Matt Dawson)*

May 2012 at Community Christian Church. My wife of twenty-four years, Angela (second from right), a beautiful, brilliant woman who is tough and demanding. My oldest daughter, Aubrey (right), who has grown into a highly principled fighter. Her nickname is Chili Bean. My youngest daughter, Austen (second from left), nickname Beetlejuice, is a technology whiz and a somewhat goofy little comedian. When you look at this picture you see the strength of America—the family. However, two-parent families represent only 28 percent of the black community. Where did we go so wrong and is it too late to restore this foundation of a successful society? I don't believe so, which is why I remain a guardian of the republic. *(West family photo)*

and bear arms is, as a last resort, to protect themselves against tyranny in government."

If we are to live up to the governing principles our founders established, then we have a mighty responsibility to preserve the power of the individual citizen. We must resist government's constant fearmongering and exploitation of our sympathies, which cause us to gradually and imperceptibly surrender individual sovereignty and liberty, drip by drip. For as Benjamin Franklin warned, "those who would give up an essential liberty for temporary security, deserve neither liberty or security."

Our own Civil War was fought to ensure we did indeed hold these truths of our Declaration of Independence to be self-evident, and we must forever defend that legacy against countless challenges, foreign and domestic. It is the latter that is most threatening. For as Abraham Lincoln said, "America will never be destroyed from the outside. If we falter and lose our freedoms, it will be because we destroyed ourselves."

This is why, more than ever, I will stand as a conservative guardian of our republic. I clearly see the dangers ahead as we gradually loosen the ties that bind us and slip away from our governing principles. I do not believe I am alone, but I will stand alone if I must.

Some would say America has failed, that the promise for which she once stood no longer exists. I believe that promise is greater than ever, but we must, as a nation, recommit to restoring it for the next generation. We can ill afford to cast aside the foundation on which this great nation was established.

We are constantly bombarded with propaganda saying America is done and our country needs to be fundamentally transformed. My answer? Nuts! Where is the flaw in individual sovereignty? Who would say liberty and freedom are passé?

Ronald Reagan reminded us, "Freedom is never more than one generation away from extinction. We didn't pass it to our children in the bloodstream. It must be fought for, protected, and handed on for them to do the same, or one day we will spend our sunset years telling our children and our children's children what it was once like in the United States where men were free." We must all join the fifty-six signers of the Declaration of Independence and take a sacred oath to preserve individual sovereignty for our children and grandchildren.

Yet however strong our nation is within, we will forever face enemies from without. Though the goal of all men should be to live in peace, our founders understood that peace was not always possible. In the preamble of the Constitution, they clearly tasked the federal government with providing "for the common defense," the fifth governing principle.

The preponderance of constitutional duties for Congress as detailed in Article I, Section 8, are defense-related. If we have a limited government, it must recognize its preeminent responsibility is national defense. If that government is fiscally responsible, it must properly allocate funds to its vital task of maintaining an appropriate force, not bribing the public with the public's treasury. To secure a thriving free market and trade, government must protect the sea lanes of commerce so that produced goods and services can be traded with allies and partners.

We must ensure Americans will be safe and protected whenever they venture abroad, for as Justice John Jay stated well before the advent of ecotourism, spring break getaways, and luxury cruises, "the safety of the people, the regard of the individual freedom and sovereignty is paramount, not just at home, but wherever an American may travel."

Defense of our nation cannot be only reactive, it must be proactive. George Washington knew this when he said, "Against the insidious wiles of foreign influence . . . the jealousy of a free people ought to be constantly awake; since history and experience prove that foreign influence is one of the most baneful foes of Republican Government."

This is a delicate dance. In today's world we are far more globally connected through commerce and technology. We must have a proactive foreign policy that promotes American interests without embroiling us in foreign exploits and ventures that erode our standing.

Providing for the common defense is impossible without good care and gratitude for those who serve. In my lifetime I have personally seen fellow Americans wrongly aim derision at those returning from the battlefield rather than at those politicians in Washington who sent them there in the first place.

As George Washington stated, "The willingness with which our young people are likely to serve in any war, no matter how justified, shall be directly proportional to how they perceive veterans of earlier wars were treated and appreciated by our nation." Never forget that our nation sleeps peacefully at night because rough men and women stand ready to do violence on her behalf.

The sixth and final governing principle enables America to be the "shining city on a hill" for all the world to see. The essence of who we are as Americans, who our Founding Fathers established us to be, was stated clearly in the Declaration of Independence—our certain unalienable rights are *endowed by our Creator.*

America was founded upon a Judeo-Christian faith heritage, not one specific religion. After all, it was for religious freedom that Europeans first came to our shores. Whether they were Pilgrims or Puritans, Protestants, Lutherans, Catholics, or even among the few dozen Jews who arrived at "New Amsterdam" in 1654, they all shared a belief in God. And however they worshipped, they all recognized that our fundamental rights, along with our fundamental understanding of morality, come from Him.

So often we hear certain people complain and demand "separation of church and state" as if it were written into our laws. But that phrase does not appear in any of our founding documents: not the Declaration of Independence, the Federalist Papers, or the Constitution.

The idea of "separation of church and state" was discussed by Thomas Jefferson in a letter to the Danbury Baptist Association in Connecticut, referring to the First Amendment's assertion that "Congress shall make no law respecting an establishment of religion." The idea was to prevent the creation of a head of state who was also the head of the church, as was the case in England. There would be no national religion, nor would we prohibit the free exercise of any religion. Jefferson's exact words were: "I contemplate with sovereign reverence that act of the whole American people which declared that their legislature should 'make no law respecting an establishment of religion, or prohibiting the free exercise thereof,' thus building a wall of separation between Church & State."

Unfortunately, the loud and secular liberal Left wants us to believe that separation of church and state means actually separating America from its faith heritage, all in the name of political correctness and some absurd definition of tolerance. But our founders understood that without the moral compass of God to guide us, our nation would quickly run aground. "Those people who will not be governed by God will be ruled by tyrants," said William Penn.

This moral compass is in part what makes our nation exceptional. Thomas Paine recognized that when he said, "The cause of America is in a great measure the cause of all mankind." It is a cause we must ever renew, for it underscores everything we do for our citizens and our fellow men.

Limited government, fiscal responsibility, a free market, individual sovereignty, a strong national defense, and an understanding that all our freedoms come ultimately from God—these are the governing principles bequeathed by our Founding Fathers, and they also form the basis of the conservative ethos. It is for this ethos I have fought and will continue to fight.

Chapter 6

PILLARS OF CONSERVATIVE THOUGHT

✫　✫　✫　✫　✫　✫　✫　✫　✫　✫　✫　✫

Nothing creates jobs faster than . . . when
people use the food stamps.
　　　—US REPRESENTATIVE NANCY PELOSI (D-CA)

In politics, stupidity is not a handicap.
　　　　　　　　　　　—NAPOLEON BONAPARTE

'VE ALWAYS believed conservatism is based on simple common sense, which, as the first statement above shows, seems to be in shorter and shorter supply on the Left. But as Emperor Napoleon pointed out, that's really nothing new.

In February 2011 I was a new member of the United States House of Representatives, having been sworn in a few weeks earlier. After a long day, I was with my chief of staff, Jonathan Blyth, at a favorite Chinese restaurant in the District of Columbia, chowing down on egg rolls and crispy General Tso's chicken, when my chief took a call on his cell phone. The subject seemed serious, and

Jonathan's tone was solemn. He said, "I will discuss this with the congressman and get back to you, as he is right here with me."

Doggone, I figured I hadn't been in Congress long enough to wreck things, so what was going on? Well, the call was from the American Conservative Union, and they had asked if I would be the keynote speaker for their flagship event, the Conservative Political Action Conference, CPAC 2011. In conservative circles the event is a pretty big deal, with nearly the entire who's who list of past and current conservative leaders appearing during the four-day conference. I was of course honored to be invited. But the interesting part was that the invitation came on Tuesday night and the conference started on Thursday. They wanted me to speak in just four days, on Saturday. I told Jonathan to call back and let them know we accepted the invitation. As we continued with our dinner, it slowly sank in what had just happened. I must admit, I did not sleep well that evening as I pondered what I would say.

The next day I observed the news surrounding CPAC and looked for a theme I could develop. It had been a very successful midterm election for conservatives, and I certainly wanted to elaborate on that and congratulate those who had worked so hard. However, I also wanted to share key policy thoughts to help us begin to focus our efforts.

I sensed that we conservatives had to do a better job

of demonstrating why our principles of governance were superior to the alternatives being offered. I saw an internal struggle to define conservatism and its components. There were those people who wanted to discuss only certain aspects of conservatism but steer clear of others. It seemed to me we were fighting about yesterday when we should be thinking about tomorrow. And then, bam! I had it! The theme would be "The Dawn of a New America," and I would refer to Ronald Reagan's brilliant campaign advertisement "It's morning in America."

To describe a new dawn and how to achieve it, I chose to speak about the three pillars of conservative thought, principles, and ideals. Now I'll give you a tip. If you want to skip ahead, you can go watch the video of the entire speech online. But I hope you'll hang out with me here so we can review the theme together.

So far in this book we've examined the philosophical foundation for America. We've delved into the vision of the Founding Fathers and illuminated their governing principles as they established these United States of America. Now it's time to talk specifically about modern conservative thought and the three pillars that support it.

The first pillar is effective and efficient conservative government. Jefferson's words, when he said, "most bad government results from too much government," ring true with every modern conservative. He was absolutely correct. I challenge anyone to show me where expansive government has been beneficial to a society and its citizens. On the contrary, history is full of examples of this failure. When I listen to the news or read certain economic pundits, I'm amazed at how they continue to harp on the same tired talking point, "We need to spend more money."

I'm sick of hearing about government investments. Let's call it what it is: government spending! By the time you're reading this book, I presume our country will have eclipsed seventeen trillion dollars in debt and be on its way to another record annual deficit. We have had trillion-dollar-plus deficits for the past four years, and you're telling me we need to spend more? Our elected officials complain about a silly 3 percent reduction in the growth of spending—nothing's being cut, it's simply not growing as much—instead of wholeheartedly assessing the size and scope of government.

Entire government agencies have not met their intended missions and are failing in the execution of their tasks—particularly their most important task of being good stewards of the American taxpayers' dollar. We are spending billions of dollars on redundant, duplicative, and ineffective government programs, yet it seems the only thing in nature that's truly eternal is a government program.

We saw the Obama administration create a new health-care entitlement program that the American people did not request. What Americans want is more jobs, yet at this writing, there are thirty-five million Americans unemployed, underemployed, or just plain discouraged.

This monstrous health-care law creates almost 160 new government agencies and bureaucracies and countless new regulations that most people, including its authors, cannot comprehend or explain.

Have we not learned our lessons about government meddling in the private sector? In 1977 President Jimmy Carter's Community Reinvestment Act inserted the federal government into the mortgage industry. The result was the creation of toxic subprime mortgages and government-sponsored hotbeds of mismanagement such as Fannie Mae and Freddie Mac, nefarious financial practices resulting from the repeal of the Glass-Steagall Act, and finally a financial meltdown in 2008. How long will it be until the Patient Protection and Affordable Care Act decimates our economy?

I say not long, because as of this writing, it's already taking its toll, especially on small business owners. The health-care law is nothing more than a tax law, thanks to Chief Justice Roberts and the justices who voted with him. The "Individual Mandate Tax" joins the twenty other taxes in the law, of which eight had already taken effect in 2013, before the act was fully implemented.

Our Founding Fathers were well aware that government expansion never has a happy ending, as they had experienced firsthand an intrusive and invasive government. The result was excessive taxation to support the whims of the crown. Today it's no different, as we're told to pay our "fair share" for the sole purpose of making government more bloated than it already is, against both our wishes and our best interests.

There are some who say President Obama won election (twice) and should be allowed to do as he wishes. To that I respond with the words of Jefferson: "I think myself that we have more machinery of government than is necessary, too many parasites living on the labor of the industrious."

So what is the policy answer? We must no longer use the tax code as a weapon to fund ideological folly. We must move toward a flat tax system. In the meantime we reform our individual tax code to include only two tax brackets: a top level at 20 to 25 percent and a lower level at 15 percent. Everyone needs to have skin in this game. We should leave in place only two deductions: mortgage interest and charitable contributions. We should eliminate capital gains, death, and dividend taxes. Finally, to encourage business to stay on our shores, our corporate/business tax rate should be reduced to between 22 and 25 percent and loopholes and deductions eliminated.

Along with tax reform must come a true, dedicated effort to make government effective and efficient. Above all, the federal government must stop being a venture capitalist—no more risky "investments" with taxpayer dollars. We should roll back the federal budget to the 2006 level and maintain it there until we get our annual deficits under control. We must analyze the scope of government with laser-guided precision, eliminate automatic annual increases in the budget, and start from zero each year.

And instead of producing a string of continuing budget resolutions generally passed under some sort of emergency shutdown threat or other manufactured crisis, how about producing a *real* budget on time? Finally, while current federal government spending is close to 25 percent of our GDP, it must be capped at 20 percent, and the cap signed into law.

And that, ladies and gentlemen, is how we ensure effective and efficient government, the first pillar of conservatism. Not sure why others have so much difficulty figuring it out . . .

The second pillar of conservatism, and the one I spent most of my adult life protecting, is peace through vigilance, resolve, and strength. As I sit here writing, the television is tuned in to Fox News and I'm listening to a *Wall Street Journal* report addressing the North Korean threat and our nation's response to it. I am unfortunately reminded of Sir Edmund Burke's words: "All that is necessary for evil to triumph is for good men to do nothing."

In 2011 North Korea sank a South Korean naval vessel and fired an artillery barrage onto a South Korean island—and we did nothing. Now it is 2013, North Korea is threatening nuclear war, the Muslim Brotherhood controls Egypt, Syria is in chaos, Iran's nuclear capability and regional hegemonic dominance grows, and we're doing nothing. We are certainly not showing resolve.

Peace, and I mean real peace, begins with courageous leaders who are willing to identify and define our enemies and their objectives. Political correctness has no place in our national security strategy. Currently we have an administration more focused on integrating openly gay and lesbian troops and allowing women into ground combat arms billets than owning up to its constitutional responsibility as it applies to national security. The administration is more comfortable combating global warming and climate change than finding the terrorists who killed a US ambassador, two former US Navy SEALs, and another American in Benghazi.

America cannot afford a Neville Chamberlain–esque security strategy that depends on the benevolence of despots, dictators, autocrats, and theocrats. I hate to remind everyone, but there are only two ways to end a war: you either win or lose. Quitting and going home because of a campaign pledge simply serves to embolden your enemies and abandon your allies.

I know a thing or two about war, and I can tell you there are only two ways to get your enemies off the battlefield: you kill them or imprison them—and that doesn't mean reading them Miranda rights and getting them all lawyered up. Terrorists do not deserve our constitutional rights, and to pretend that granting those rights gets us respect from our enemies is the most asinine concept I have ever heard.

If we cannot adapt to the changing twenty-first-century battlefield with its nonstate, nonuniformed belligerents operating without respect for borders and boundaries, we are setting ourselves up for future attacks. We must have a completely different strategy for deployment and engagement against this flexible and fluid enemy. It's time that we moved away from the idea of a large, standing "forward deployed" force, where units and resources are permanently stationed outside of the United States, to a rapid-response "power projection" force that uses our strategic and operational ability to deploy as our greatest asset.

We must stop with the nation building and focus more on strike operations. We need a strategy across all our geographic areas of responsibility that provides the correct mix of forces, capacity, and capability to deny the enemy sanctuary, cut off his flow of men and material, win the information war, and cordon off his ability to extend his sphere of influence.

This does not mean we have to double or triple the size of our defense budget. It's about building the most efficient and effective military, one that doesn't stress our men and women in uniform with excessive combat tours of duty and that adequately cares for our veterans and military families.

We can secure the blessings of liberty by providing for the common defense. But it all starts with resolute leadership—something we have been sorely lacking for quite some time. I often reflect that during the 2012 presidential election, for the first time in seventy-seven years we did not have either a sitting president or vice president or a single candidate who had ever served our country in uniform. How different would our stance and standing in the world be today if we had? How differently would our enemies view us now if we firmly stood on our second pillar of peace through strength?

Finally, the third (and I believe the most important) pillar of conservatism. It is perhaps the least tangible, but it sets our nation apart from the rest of the world: our traditional American values. These values are the reason why so many have risked their lives to set foot on our shores and take part in this grand venture of liberty.

But to join in this grand venture, we must come together as one people and share the most basic and common bond: our language. Those who immigrated to this nation once relished the fact it was a great melting pot, where anyone from anywhere could become an American. Now Americans appear so over the top in support of multiculturalism that we're in danger of "Balkanizing" our own country. We are making American culture subservient, and, well, that dog won't hunt. This is America, and we have a sign on the front door that says (in English), "Open, come on in."

Our traditional American values also include a respect for God, faith, and worship. We have no national religion—our founders didn't want one, and no one is suggesting one now. But we do have a national heritage of faith. There's a good reason our national motto is "In God we trust." In the words of John Adams, "Our Constitution was made only for a moral and religious people. It is wholly inadequate to the government of any other."

But lately it seems we must fight to reclaim this faith heritage. Why? These values are a fundamental part of our nation, written into its DNA. A denial of faith is a denial of America. Is that what fundamental transformation means?

It is not a question of separating church and state. It is about ensuring we don't separate faith from the individual. We welcome all faiths in America, but our coexistence must not come at the expense of our American values. As I have said many times, when tolerance becomes a one-way street, it leads to cultural suicide. And as far as I'm concerned, American cultural values shall never be subjugated to any other so long as I have air in my lungs.

Our heritage of faith points to our Creator as the source of the rights we are granted not just in this country but during our existence on earth. The first of those rights is the right to life. I may not speak for all conservatives on this subject, but I will certainly speak my mind. I fully support the right to life for our unborn. What does it say of our better angels if we deny the fundamental first right as articulated by John Locke and Thomas Jefferson? I believe neither late-term abortion nor abortion as birth control reflects our true values. Having a baby is certainly not a punishment.

In early April 2013, a woman speaking on behalf of Planned Parenthood before a Florida legislature subcommittee was asked a simple question: "Does a child that survives an abortion still deserve to die?" Her response was that the decision was between the patient and the doctor. You must understand that she was referring to the mother as the patient. When challenged again and asked if the surviving baby was the patient, the woman could not respond.

I know this is a sensitive and complex topic. But each of us must ask, is abortion reflective of our best system of values? The winning argument in *Roe v. Wade* determined the right of privacy was *implied* in the Bill of Rights and by Amendments 1, 3, 4, 5, 9, and 14. The US Supreme Court ruled a woman has a right to terminate her pregnancy up to ninety days after conception. Why ninety days? What happens magically at ninety-one? Has any human being been able to skip those first ninety days before birth? And is individual privacy of greater value than the unalienable right to life? I'm not sure the federal government should be the one to answer this question, but I am certain each of us must.

The final American value we must preserve is the family. Our country needs strong families to form the building blocks of our society. Wherever the family unit has been weakened, we see detrimental effects. In the black community, where only 30 percent of children have a mother and a father in their home, soaring crime, unemployment, and poor classroom performance are the results. When the fabric of our families unravels, our nation weakens. Stronger families ensure a stronger America.

Our American values matter. They define us, and they define the legacy we pass on to the next generation. These pillars of thought have blessed us with the greatest country the world has ever known. It was George Washington who said, "We are either a united people or we are not. If the former, let us in all matter of general concern act as a nation which has national objects to promote and a national character to support. If we are not, let us no longer act a farce by pretending to it."

Now is the time to make a stand. We must do as Abraham Lincoln said and put our feet in the right place and stand firm. We must stand firm if we are to secure the dawn of a new America. We must stand firm if we are to be guardians of this republic. If we falter and lose this great blessing called the United States, it will be because we turned our back on our past and destroyed ourselves. But we can prevail. We know what the light is; we can be that shining city upon a hill. Let us be what our Founding Fathers hoped we would be and what our children and grandchildren need us to be. Let us be Americans.

Chapter 7

CONFLICTING PHILOSOPHIES OF GOVERNANCE

✶ ✶ ✶ ✶ ✶ ✶ ✶ ✶ ✶ ✶ ✶

*Socialism is a philosophy of failure, the
creed of ignorance, and the gospel of envy,
its inherent virtue is the equal sharing of
misery.*

—SIR WINSTON CHURCHILL

*Socialists ignore the side of man that is the
spirit. They can provide you shelter, fill
your belly with bacon and beans, treat you
when you're ill, all the things guaranteed to
a prisoner or a slave. They don't understand
that we also dream.*

—PRESIDENT RONALD REAGAN

*The problem with socialism is that you
eventually run out of other people's money.*

—BARONESS MARGARET THATCHER

Less than a week before the 2008 presidential election, then candidate Barack Hussein Obama proclaimed, "We are just five days away from fundamentally transforming the United States of America." The crowd went into a frenzy of cheering and screaming, just as there had been instances of fainting spells and hysteria at previous Obama speeches. What still amazes me to this day, however, is that no one ever asked what it means to "fundamentally transform America." What was so wrong with the governing fundamentals of America that they needed to be transformed? After all, the Founding Fathers gave us a brilliant system whereby we could institute amendments to our law of the land, the Constitution.

Did anyone ever ask, "What is it, Senator Obama, that you feel needs transforming? Is it something about our system of checks and balances, separation of powers, the free market economy, individual rights, or constitutional limits on government? What exactly needs to be thrown out and remade?"

Why was it that even the ostensibly unbiased media did not challenge the young first-term senator on his statement? Was it perhaps because they knew the answer and wanted to conceal it? Could it be that even our own free press was complicit in hiding the truth from the people for some nefarious gain?

Who can say? Any attempt to challenge Senator Obama was met with charges of racism—a practice that continues today with ever greater absurdity from that bastion of rational reporting, MSNBC. According to Lawrence O'Donnell, comparing Obama's frequent rounds of golf to Tiger Woods's is racist. To Chris Matthews, reminding people of Obama's Chicago roots is racist. And according to Touré Neblett, using the word *angry* when criticizing Obama is racist.

As I mentioned before, during times of universal deceit, telling the truth becomes a revolutionary act. So in this chapter, it's time for a revolutionary act: to define truthfully what the "fundamental transformation of America" means.

If we're fundamentally transforming America, it must mean we're moving toward the opposite of limited government, fiscal responsibility, individual sovereignty, free markets, strong national defense, and traditional values. But where did this shift come from, and how can we alert our republic as to how dangerous this new direction is? I am also troubled by a deeper question: do the American people even care they may be surrendering the country bequeathed to them, that a legacy of freedom could be lost forever?

To start, let's take a look at where this "fundamental

transformation" has brought our country so far. Since President Obama's inauguration in 2009, nearly every objective measurement shows things have been fundamentally transformed . . . for the worse.

allenbwest.com Data Card			
Economic Indicator	January 2009	November 14, 2013	Change
Unemployed Americans	12 million	11.3 million	-5.8%
Unemployment rate	7.8%	7.3%	-6.8%
Workforce Participation Rate	65.7%	63.4%	-3.6%
Gas per gallon	$1.84	$3.19	+73%
Federal debt	$10.6 trillion	$17.1 trillion	+61%
Debt per person	$34,731	$54,066	+$19,335
Food stamp recipients	32 million	47.7 million	+49%
Home values	$172,100	$199,200	+15.7%
Americans in poverty	39.8 million	49.1 million	+9.3 million (+23%)
Health insurance premiums	$13,375	$16,351	+22%
Misery index	7.8	8.5	+9%

During his presidential campaign, Ronald Reagan asked a simple question of America: "Are you better off than you were four years ago?" It sure would be refreshing if someone in the mainstream media would do a piece on what the fundamental transformation of America meant in 2008, what it means for us today, and what it will mean for our future.

To understand this fundamental transformation, it's helpful to examine once again the prevailing models of political thought at the time of our Founding Fathers. We must revisit Jean-Jacques Rousseau.

Rousseau believed compassion for his fellow man, and in particular for those less fortunate, was the greatest of virtues. He didn't care for the recognition of distinctions among people, as he felt it led to inequality and divisiveness. For Rousseau it was better to view people through the prism of their good intentions rather than their appearance or achievements. He firmly believed in the good nature of man, but he saw fundamental problems in social institutions. In other words, Rousseau thought society was to blame for the corruption of the pure individual.

Contrary to John Locke, Rousseau maintained that the social institution that brought about the most corruption was private property. He viewed it as a destructive, impulsive, and self-absorbed institution that rewarded greed and luck. The bottom line for Rousseau was that inequality grew out of the fact that some people would produce and earn more than others. Because talents and abilities were not distributed equally, the original balance that existed in the state of nature would be altered and the resulting inequality would create conflict. Rousseau's vision of a civil society was one where no one had the "right" to rise above the general level of subsistence without everyone else's consent.

Herein lies the conflict between the political philosophies of Locke and Rousseau, between the classical liberal and the first radical liberal. Locke believed the individual had the unalienable rights of life, liberty, and estate. Where Locke promoted the minimization of the state/government, Rousseau wanted the opposite. Rousseau proposed a fundamental transformation of the relationship between the individual citizen and the state. For Locke the state of nature promoted freedom, but for Rousseau it promoted subordination and required a system of indoctrination to convince individuals that the public interest is greater and truly better for their personal interests.

Rousseau called for a merging of state and individual, in which each individual gives up his right to control his life in exchange for an equal voice in setting the ground rules of society. He advocated surrendering individual rights to a new moral and collective body, with one will, which was a fundamental change from the belief in the sovereignty of individuals and their indomitable spirits and personal will. In America we do "hold these truths to be self-evident that all men are created equal because they are endowed with certain unalienable rights." But as Rousseau sought to establish a different type of social contract, he completely redefined the relationship between the individual and the state.

While Jefferson wrote of the "consent of the governed," Rousseau believed individuals had to consent to the "general will," which was essentially whatever everyone else wanted. When forced to obey the general will, people were actually obeying themselves. Rousseau asserted that individuals would voluntarily transfer their personal rights to the community in return for security of life and property.

But this system has a downside. As Edward Younkins explained in his book *Capitalism and Commerce*, "The result is that all powers, persons, and their rights are under control and direction of the entire community. This means that no one can do anything without the consent of all. Such universal dependency eliminates the possibility of individual achievement. Life is a gift made conditional by the state. All power is transferred to a central authority."

Needless to say, our founders completely rejected Rousseau's ideas. When the general will is always right, the individual's ideas, values, and goals mean nothing—a point of view thoroughly incompatible with the founders' vision.

The Founding Fathers could not agree with the theory that freedom was a result of obedience, and equality of servitude. They were appalled by the concept of a universal dependency and the subjugation of the individual will.

The disturbing aspect of Rousseau's theories was his perspective on opposition. Once the general will makes its decision, Rousseau permitted no disobedience. Even if individuals disagree with the decision, their will must be subordinated, because anyone who disagrees with the general will must be simply mistaken! Certainly writer Andrew Sullivan was echoing Rousseau in his January

2012 *Newsweek* cover story, "Why Are Obama's Critics So Dumb?" where he asserts that anyone, conservative or liberal, who criticizes the president is simply wrong.

Our Founding Fathers did not adopt Rousseau's philosophy of governance, thank God, but others, such as the French Jacobins, did, plunging their country into a brutal civil war and revolution in the late 1700s that led to the Reign of Terror. Those groups who adopted Rousseauian philosophy always expressed an exuberant yet quite deceptive concept of social humanitarianism, where violent means justified supposedly peaceful ends.

In Germany in the early 1800s, Georg Wilhelm Friedrich Hegel picked up the mantle of Rousseau and expanded on his theories to assert that it was only through social institutions that one could realize oneself. Hegel believed the state represented the high point of human history, through which the sublime spirit used individuals as its instrument. In Hegel's mind the coercive powers of the state could be legitimately—and paradoxically—exercised to achieve individual freedom. The antidemocratic themes of Rousseau may have been hummed by Hegel, but they received a full-throated yeehaw from Karl Heinrich Marx.

The idea of communism or "communal living" was not new. For many thousands of years, humans had been living together in communities because it provided many advantages over solo hunting and gathering. But to Karl Marx, communism was the natural and preferred result of "historical materialism." In Marx's view, capitalists squeeze profit from an exploited working class, which causes a class struggle, igniting a revolution, and eventually culminating in sunny communism.

Commissioned by the Communist League in 1848, Marx and Friedrich Engels's book *The Communist Manifesto* was a criticism of capitalism intended to build enthusiasm for a revolution among the working class. The fundamental result of the revolution would be the elimination of capitalism and the establishment of a national collective economy and nationalized welfare state, along with ownership and control of the major means of production. There were two collateral objectives as well: setting people free from the prison of material dependence, and the creation of the secular state.

Key aspects of the philosophy of governance known as Marxism included the definitive class structure divided between the "bourgeoisie," those owning most of the wealth and the means of production, and the "proletariat," or the working class—terms that fit nicely with the modern-day "1 percent" and "99 percent" labels used by our current White House administration.

In addition, Marxism incorporated the concept of wealth distribution: "From each according to his ability, to each according to his needs." This social egalitarianism would be attained through a central government authority, a political entity that directed and enforced compliance with the general will.

A few months back, I took some heavy flak for suggesting that members of the Congressional Progressive Caucus share more governing philosophy with other communist countries than with our own. On that note I'd like to present eight of the ten planks of *The Communist Manifesto* so you can decide for yourself if I was right.

1. *Abolition of private property in land and application of all rents of land to public purpose.* You only need to talk to US representatives from western states about the immense expansion of the federal government and consider how many energy resources are located on "public" lands in America. This was a policy established by President Theodore Roosevelt, who redefined himself as a Progressive candidate (more on this in a bit).

2. *A heavy progressive or graduated income tax.* Prior to 1913 America used a consumption-based system of taxation related to goods and services purchased. Then in 1913 we created the individual income tax, with a top rate one hundred years ago of just 7 percent. Today the top marginal tax rate is 39.6 percent, and we hear the drumbeat of the rich paying their "fair share," "economic equality," "economic patriotism" . . . hmm, sounds an awful lot like "from

each according to his ability, to each according to his needs."

3.   *Abolition of all rights of inheritance.* This one is easy. Ever heard of the "death tax" or, as some term it, the "estate tax"? Estate (property) was one of the unalienable rights, endowed by our Creator, identified by Locke. But I guess in a secular state the state is the creator, as Rousseau promoted, and individual accumulation has to be minimized.

4.   *Confiscation of the property of emigrants and rebels.* Need to be careful here, because I believe one of our First Amendment rights is to petition our grievances to government. Heck, that was the whole point of the Declaration of Independence. But here's the key point: who decides what constitutes a rebel? the IRS? local government? There are thousands of cases of "eminent domain" where the local, state, or federal government takes property from one private owner and hands it to another, simply because the government thinks the other party will make better use of it.

5.   *Centralization of credit in the hands of the state by means of a national bank with state capital and an exclusive monopoly.* During Woodrow Wilson's presidency, at about the same time that personal in-

come tax was created, the Federal Reserve Bank was founded. Another brilliant idea? A national bank, which conducts monetary policy irrespective of overall national fiscal policy—how's that working for us? It's a reckless approach for short-term gain at the expense of future generations. Just check out Ben Bernanke and his "quantitative easing" policies of printing money and lowering interest rates, which create in effect an artificially robust economy . . . using taxpayer dollars. It may look fine now, but this house of cards cannot stand forever. Reality has a nasty way of biting.

6. *Centralization of the means of communication and transportation in the hands of the state.* We have the Federal Communications Commission, established in 1934 under progressive Democrat President Franklin Delano Roosevelt, and the US Department of Transportation established in 1967 under Democrat President Lyndon Baines Johnson. Anyone see a trend here?

7. *Extension of factories and instruments of production owned by the state, the bringing into cultivation of wastelands, and the improvement of the soil generally in accordance with a common plan.* This would be the nationalizing of production and the in-

jection of the state into the free market/private sector, à la the Community Reinvestment Act, Patient Protection and Affordable Care Act, Dodd-Frank Wall Street Reform and Consumer Protection Act, and auto manufacturer and bank bailouts, as well as the creation of the Departments of Agriculture, Commerce, Labor, and the Interior; the Bureaus of Land Management, Reclamation, and Mines; and the National Park Service.

8. *Free education for all children in government schools.* The US Department of Education has practically become a propaganda arm of the federal government, and a highly politicized teachers' union, the National Education Association, controls the education process. Remember, it was Rousseau who advocated state education to enlighten the populace as to what the "community" or the "general will" wanted. This Rousseauian view has permeated our colleges and universities and explains why there are even educators against school choice, charter schools, and home schooling. Don't forget that your taxes are used to pay for these "public schools"—another means by which the state can minimize the property of some in order to promote the design of the state. Over the last thirty years, public education has gradually morphed into public indoctrination.

There is one "unofficial" plank that becomes essential in the Marxist/socialist movement: state control of the press. To control the population, you must control the message, which reinforces the "general will" that must be obeyed. What a surprise that liberal outlets like MSNBC employ former Obama administration officials who are perfectly placed to ensure every story gets the preferred progressive spin. A complicit national media willingly allows the state to control the narrative by focusing on those stories that fit the state's agenda and ignoring other perspectives.

Did our founders advocate for no government? Absolutely not. They were far from anarchists. But what they did construct was a system of limited government with defined roles and responsibilities. Following Locke's design, they wrote the Constitution to place restraint on government; they did not adopt Rousseau's plan to place the restraint on the individual. Our founders embraced Locke's classical liberalism, and their beliefs built the foundation of modern conservatism.

So what is today's liberalism?

First of all, contemporary or "postmodern" liberalism isn't liberalism in the classic sense at all, because today it has no true relationship to the ideals of Locke. It grows from the theories of Rousseau, who gave birth to Marxism and socialism—clearly the antithesis of our American constitutionalism. That's why we were told there was a fundamental transformation a-comin'. It's happening right under our noses.

But I keep coming back to one simple question: why is the danger of progressive liberalism so difficult for people to comprehend? It's obviously not being taught, at least not without some blatant bias. To answer that question, there is one more mystery to explore: what the heck is a progressive?

Most historians agree Progressivism was a political reform movement that began in the late nineteenth century and continued through the first decades of the twentieth century. The movement counted among its members leading intellectuals, social reformers, and political leaders such as John Dewey, Theodore Woolsey, John Burgess, Herbert Croly, Charles Merriam, Woodrow Wilson, and Theodore Roosevelt. Progressives wanted to address the economic, political, and cultural issues that had arisen from the changes of the Industrial Revolution and the growth of modern capitalism in America. Individually they may have differed in their assessments and solutions for these problems, but they all agreed that government had to be more actively engaged at every level, thereby departing from our traditional notion of limited government.

Early in the twentieth century, American progressive ideology was influential in shaping policies such as the direct elections of senators, open primaries, and the ability of the electorate to bypass the legislature with initiatives, referendums, and recalls. Since an expanded government needs revenue, Progressives were influential in the passage of the Sixteenth Amendment: the progressive income tax.

It's easy to see the correlation between progressivism, Marxism, and socialism, and many historians believe progressivism was simply an exercise in "rebranding" in order to make European Marxist and socialist ideas more palatable to Americans. Today you can call it socialism, communism, progressivism, or "statism"—the term used by constitutional scholar, radio host, and "Great One" Mark Levin—the fundamentals are the same.

Whether out of good intentions or a conscious repudiation of America's founding principles, there can be no doubt that the followers of progressivism transformed American politics. But no matter the intent, the result is that progressivism, now modified and assimilated into contemporary liberalism, is the predominant view presented in America today by means of education, media, popular culture, and politics. This does not mean it represents the perspective of the majority, but it is the prevailing perspective being promoted.

What does that mean for our country?

Our classical liberal founders believed in the natural rights of man and the law of nature, as bestowed by our Creator. Jefferson wrote that we are obliged "to respect those rights in others which we value in ourselves."

But Progressive John Dewey said, "Freedom is not something that individuals have as a ready-made possession." For Dewey our freedom was nothing more than a quaint ideal, and he stated: "Natural rights and natural liberties exist only in the kingdom of mythological social zoology." That's quite a departure from the fundamental concept of unalienable rights as laid out in the Declaration of Independence. You see, for progressives there are no permanent standards of rights. Instead they support the idea of historical relativity.

The original constitution written for the Commonwealth of Massachusetts in 1780 states that "the body-politic is formed by a voluntary association of individuals: It is a social compact, by which the whole people covenants with each citizen, and each citizen with the whole people, that all shall be governed by certain laws for the common good."

But less than 150 years later, Progressives were rejecting the idea of a social compact. Political scientist Charles Merriam (no relation to the dictionary Merriams) wrote, "The individualistic ideas of the 'natural right' school of political theory, endorsed in the Revolution, are discredited and repudiated." Merriam believed natural rights had "no proper place in politics."

As such, today's progressives have no use for religion either. And why should they? After all, who needs God when, as Hegel said, "the state is the divine idea as it exists on earth." Is it any surprise that when there was a vote to reinsert the word *God* into the Democratic platform at the 2012 convention the proposal was met with boos and disdain? I guess that's what it means to fundamentally transform America.

For the Founding Fathers, the expressed purpose of government was to protect private individuals and their industrial nature. According to Jefferson, "A wise and frugal government, which shall restrain men from injuring one another, which shall leave them otherwise free to regulate their own pursuits of industry and improvement, and shall not take from the mouth of labor the bread it has earned. This is the sum of good government."

But Progressive President Woodrow Wilson completely disagreed. As part of Rousseau's intellectual political elite, Wilson believed Jefferson's type of government was unjust, "because it leaves men to the mercy of predatory corporations. Without government management of these corporations, the poor would be destined to indefinite victimization by the wealthy"—which sounds an awful lot like Marx and Engels to me.

I don't deny there is a need for some market regulation. A great example is the Glass-Steagall Act of 1933, which kept a prudent separation between commercial and investment banking. Unfortunately Glass-Steagall was repealed during the Clinton administration, leading to larger banks getting involved in mortgage-backed securities—and we all know how that ended in 2008. When the state believes it should intervene in the private sector, it never ends well. We get crony capitalism and governmental venture capitalism like the Solyndra debacle, where the government invested half a billion dollars of taxpayer money in an unproven energy company only to have it go bankrupt two years later.

In terms of domestic policy, the founders wanted to encourage an independent, hardworking populace with laws and educational institutions that promoted values such as honesty, moderation, justice, patriotism, courage, frugality, and industry. As the new government sought to expand the territory of the United States with the Northwest Ordinance of 1787, it was written that "government should promote education because religion, morality, knowledge are necessary to good government and the happiness of mankind."

But for Progressives, there were two priorities of domestic policy: protecting the poor and other victims of capitalism through redistributive policies, and state control of commerce, production, manufacturing, and banking.

Regarding foreign policy, the Founding Fathers believed that the best way to defend the security and property of the people was with deterrence, not aggression. Alliances were to be sought not to engage in quarrels with other nations but solely for our own defense.

How interesting that Progressives believed in promoting the dominance of a political idea by force. In fact

Charles Merriam openly called for a policy of colonialism on a racial basis: "The Teutonic races must civilize the politically uncivilized. They must have a colonial policy. Barbaric races, if incapable, may be swept away."

In 1899 Theodore Roosevelt wrote his own vision of imperialism in his essay "Expansion and Peace," saying, "every expansion of a great civilized power means a victory for law, order, and righteousness."

A final distinction between progressive ideals and our founding principles is in the area of leadership. James Madison believed our leaders "should not be experts, but they should have the most wisdom to discern, and most virtue to pursue, the common good of the society."

In contrast, Progressives disregarded what they considered amateurism in politics. They did not believe in the liberally educated statesman. According to that view, if nineteenth-century frontiersman and soldier Davy Crockett had been born a hundred years later, he could never have been effective in Congress, because politics clearly was too complicated for a man of his common sense. Damn, they would have gotten that one wrong! Today's progressives follow in the same vein, believing that only those educated in top universities are capable of governing. Needless to say, they believe in a political elite class (and I thought they just didn't like my round-rimmed spectacles). For progressives, it's all about a strong central governing authority and an extensive bureaucratic administrative apparatus.

So here we are, America.

The Wilson period, the Franklin Roosevelt New Deal period, and the Johnson–Carter periods reflect previous eras of progressivism in America. I believe we are currently in a new and more dangerous period, one begun by George W. Bush and accelerated by Barack H. Obama. In 2008 we were just five days away from fundamentally transforming our nation. It's now five years later. Are we going to stop it?

America survived the first great battle for its soul, the Civil War. Will we be able to survive the second battle between our constitutional founding principles and those of ever-encroaching progressive statism?

I know for which I stand, and against which I fight. Do you?

PART III

CONSERVATISM IN THE BLACK COMMUNITY

Chapter 8

THE SOUL OF OUR SOULS

✷ ✷ ✷ ✷ ✷ ✷ ✷ ✷ ✷ ✷ ✷ ✷ ✷ ✷

*The Negro should acquire property, own
his own land, drive his own mule hitched
to his own wagon, milk his own cow, raise
his own crop and keep out of debt, and
when he acquired a home he became fit for a
conservative citizen.*

BOOKER T. WASHINGTON

*Boy, don't ever see your color as a handicap,
and never use it as a crutch.*

—HERMAN "BUCK" WEST SR.

In this chapter I'd like to speak to my fellow Americans who also happen to be black. There are many among the liberal Left who seem to think being black and conservative is some type of affliction, a racial anomaly that has only recently appeared in America. They could not be more wrong in their assessment, because they fail to understand the soul of our souls.

I remember back in January 2011, on day one of the 112th Congress, when I was waiting for the Congressional Black Caucus swearing-in. Boy howdy, for some people, the atmosphere could have been cut with a knife, there was that much tension and apprehension. In walked Representative John Lewis, civil rights icon, and I shook his hand. I explained how I remembered my parents voting for him and explained that I was an alumnus of Henry Grady High. He couldn't believe where I came from. You see, during the 2010 election cycle, Congressman Lewis had vocally opposed me without a clue who I really was.

My parents, Buck and Snooks, were registered Democrats, like most of my family. But regardless of party affiliation, I was raised with very conservative principles and values. Conservatism in the black community was not so much about political inclinations as it was a way of life that we called "old school." Old school was a cultural phenomenon; it put the "soul" in our souls. It was all about walking down the street and graciously greeting the old folks, because that reflected on the way your parents were raising you—and trust me, you did not want to bring shame upon your family. As with the ronin, position in the community was all about honor. Regardless of how old you were and whether your parents had passed, you carried their name and their reputation.

As I mentioned before, I never, ever wanted to disappoint my dad by not greeting my elders with sir or ma'am. After that first time, it was a whuppin' I vowed never to repeat. That lesson has stayed with me to this very day, which is why, when perfect strangers come up to me anywhere, I still address them as sir or ma'am.

Conservatism in the black community was written about as early as 1908 by Kelly Miller, the first black scholar to graduate from Johns Hopkins University and, later, dean of Howard University. In his essay titled "Radicals and Conservatives," Miller was one of the first to classify followers of Booker T. Washington as conservatives.

For the black community, the fundamental basis of conservatism, as rooted in the classical liberalism of John Locke, was individual liberty. Who better to seek true freedom and liberty than those who had suffered under the yoke of slavery? If America and the dreams of the Founding Fathers were to have any meaning, slavery had to be abolished. Once it was, the blessings of liberty would have to be secured for those who hadn't previously enjoyed them. I believe—and will gladly argue this stand against anyone—that black conservatives have always seen individual liberty as the prerequisite true justice, not government-manufactured economic or social justice. One of the premier conservative thinkers, Sir Edmund Burke, said: "Liberty has strong foundations in the people's religious faith and social institutions." Burke called these institutions the "little platoons" of society.

The little platoon of the black community is the church. Our Christian faith is based on individual freedom from sin and the personal decision to find spiritual liberty that leads to a better life here on earth and for eternity. On Sundays in America, the most conservative people can be found in black churches. But what happens to that conservatism during the rest of the week? What causes the split in our values between holy day and every day?

The roots of this dichotomy were formed in the fifty-odd years after the abolition of slavery and solidified in the contrasting viewpoints of Booker T. Washington and W. E. B. Du Bois as examined in Kelly Miller's 1908 essay.

Booker Taliaferro Washington's life was a profile in courage. Born into slavery in rural Virginia, Washington rose to great prominence and respect, received honorary degrees from Harvard University and Dartmouth College, and took tea with the queen of England. He was the first black American to appear on a US postage stamp, and a battleship was even named after him. After graduating from and later teaching at Hampton University in Virginia, he went on to found Tuskegee University in Alabama in 1881. Washington was catapulted to prominence with his powerful address delivered in 1895—the year of Frederick Douglass's death—at the Atlanta Cotton States and International Exposition.

In his address Washington entreated his fellow freed

men never to permit their grievances to overshadow their opportunities. Like Douglass, he believed strongly in the resilience, strength, and potential of black Americans based on a conservative policy of three pillars familiar to all conservatives: education, self-reliance, and entrepreneurship. Washington was a guiding light not just for black conservatism but for American conservatism.

One of my favorite personal quotes is Horace Mann's oft-paraphrased statement "Education then, beyond all other devices of human origin, is the great equalizer of the conditions of men." Washington agreed, but he also believed education was most valuable as a means of achieving practical ends, as he wrote in *Up from Slavery* in 1901: "The actual sight of a first-class house that a Negro has built is ten times more potent than pages of discussion about a house that he ought to build, or perhaps could build."

What if our nation in general and the black community specifically had had that mind-set when President Jimmy Carter came up with the Community Reinvestment Act in the late 1970s? What if we had stressed Booker T. Washington's principle of self-reliance and economic independence instead of Washington, DC's reliance on government solutions? Perhaps the United States might have avoided the subprime mortgage crisis that brought about the financial collapse in 2008.

As a true conservative, Booker T. Washington believed power for the black community would come from building an economic foundation, not by focusing on a political remedy.

Washington's greatest criticism came not from the white establishment, however, but from a fellow black man, W. E. B. Du Bois.

In contrast to Washington and his rural southern up-bringing, William Edward Burghardt Du Bois grew up in the relatively integrated north, in Massachusetts. Du Bois was the first black American to earn a doctorate from Harvard and was one of the cofounders of the NAACP.

At first the two men corresponded and sought each other's counsel frequently. The younger Du Bois endeav-ored to gain prominence among the black intelligentsia, and Washington was considered its leader. But by the time Du Bois's book *The Souls of Black Folk* was pub-lished in 1903, battle lines were drawn. Du Bois openly criticized Washington, rejected his three-pillar philoso-phy, and challenged him for the leadership of American blacks. Du Bois retracted his earlier praise of Washing-ton's speech at the Atlanta Exposition, renaming it the "Atlanta Compromise"—a pejorative label used by lib-eral progressives to this day.

Du Bois, in opposition to Washington, contended that full political rights—not economic independence—would better assist blacks in winning equality. He claimed Wash-ington was against higher education, which couldn't have been further from the truth. Washington simply recognized that a greater percentage of the black community would benefit from receiving a practical education first.

By the time of Washington's early death at age fifty-nine from hypertension, the rift between the two men was irreparable. The die would be forever cast in the black community, dividing it into two camps that still exist today. Du Bois advocated black protest, militancy, and pride, a position heavily supported then by white liberal philanthropists and today by progressive socialists. Washington advocated assimilation, practical education, and thrift—for which he was viciously attacked. He was called an "Uncle Tom," the horrible epithet used even today by those in the black community against anyone who speaks out against status quo policies.

If you visit the Library of Congress and read Booker T. Washington's papers, you'll discover an incredibly accomplished man who, without grandstanding, developed a practical plan to implement his policies. Washington wanted to build institutions to promote his three-pronged philosophy of education, self-reliance, and entrepreneurship. At the time his ideas were opposed by leftist ideologues who, although loud and vocal, produced nothing but rhetoric. Not much in the debate has changed since then.

Compare Booker T. Washington, the consummate conservative, with W. E. B. Du Bois, the radical leftist, and you can see the origins of the current conflict in our community. The soul of our souls is searching and wavering between two choices: to go back to our roots as believers in an opportunity society or to stay mired in a belief in the dependency society.

In 1908 Kelly Miller explained the conflict this way: "Radical and conservative Negroes agree as to the end in view, but differ as to the most effective means of attaining it." Despite great steps forward in desegregation and civil rights legislation over the last hundred years—including electing a black president not once but twice—we are no closer to finding agreement.

Einstein defined insanity as doing the same thing over and over again but expecting different results. Why then does the black community continue to invest all its political capital in one type of policy approach, hoping for a different result?

Would you put all your money in one type of security— or, even worse, tell your broker that is what you planned to do? Over time you'd surely be taken for granted or you'd risk losing everything—or both.

The path of W. E. B. Du Bois has not yielded profitable returns for the black community. So I say, let's go back to a practical plan of execution, with conservatism based on a useful education, self-reliance, and entrepreneurship. Let's put our faith in economic freedom, moral strength, and God. Voting rights, protests, and marches were the beginning not the end to our struggle for equality.

Some may say I'm old-fashioned or out of touch, that

my view is too old-school. Well, let me tell you what "old school" means to me.

For anyone growing up in the home of Buck and Snooks at 651 Kennesaw Avenue Northeast in Atlanta, Georgia, education was a top priority. Mom went to college at Fort Valley State. Although Dad never received more than a high school degree, he was nevertheless a fierce advocate of schooling. Education wasn't a priority for just Buck and Snooks's sons but for the entire extended family. My Aunt Brendalyn attended Morris Brown College and became an esteemed high school educator in Knoxville. My Uncle Jerome went to Tennessee State University and became a top engineer. Cousins graduated from East Tennessee State and Tennessee Tech. Yep, my folks were all about getting an education. If you didn't attend college, you'd better develop a solid skill through a trade. Education was the key that allowed you to lead a productive life rather than a dependent one. I never wanted to come home with bad grades.

My wife, Angela, and I continue Buck and Snooks's legacy. Our daughters are being brought up in a home where Dad has a bachelor's degree and two master's and Mom, the genius, has a bachelor's, an MBA, and a PhD. I received an honorary doctorate degree from Northwood University, but Angela says it still doesn't top hers. Damn! But academic achievement certainly runs in her family. Angela's brothers include a doctor, a lawyer, an engineer, a computer engineer, and a finance manager for a petroleum company.

There is no question that education—whether formal academics or practical skill-set development—unlocks the potential for greater opportunities. But I am witnessing a complete lack of appreciation for either in the black community. It's clear that schools in the inner city are failing black children, but throwing more money at the problem is not exactly the answer. I believe we need competition in the education industry, and I support school choice. I was very fortunate that both my parents invested in my education by sending me to Catholic school.

But even given my access to excellent schools, I would not have been pushed and prodded toward academic excellence were it not for my parents and my strong, supportive family. Sadly, today Angela and I are part of only about 28 percent of black households with children that have both a mother and father in the home. The black out-of-wedlock birth rate hovers around 72 percent—that's a cultural death blow. Widespread unwed motherhood was unheard of in the black community when I grew up, and it is antithetical to who we are as a people. I place much of the blame for this crisis on the "Great Society" programs of President Johnson, which I'll talk about in the next chapter, but I must offer a few more thoughts on the issue of unwed motherhood here.

It was a Democratic senator, Daniel Patrick Moynihan, who advised against providing checks to women having children out of wedlock. He warned of the break-down of the family, especially the black family, and of all the unintended consequences that would arise. Well, as Jim Nabors's Gomer Pyle character would say, "Surprise, surprise, surprise!" Moynihan's predictions came true, with devastating consequences for education and opportunities in the black community.

Marriage isn't simply important. It's *fundamental*. Children from traditional married households simply do better. That's not to say single parents and their children cannot succeed, but the odds are stacked against them. And nowhere is this more evident than in our black community.

Does anyone else find it hypocritical that progressive socialists promote choice in killing children but reject saving them through educational choice?

Why do current black elected officials turn their backs on school choice and strong families? Why do they support the progressive socialist agenda, the exact opposite of what's needed at a fundamental level to begin the restoration of the inner-city black communities? Hello, Detroit? The violence in Chicago has almost nothing to do with gun control and nearly everything to do with the rise of gangs, because we've failed to provide quality education in the inner city and destroyed the black family.

Education and family can exist only when there is respect for personal and financial responsibility and self-reliance. Mom's thrifty shopping habits, her fondness for layaway plans and the cash-only approach, were ingrained in me from a very young age. I'm still not a fancy department-store shopper and no one would ever accuse me of being fashion-conscious either! Ol' Buck conveyed other financial lessons that serve me well today. He encouraged me to read the box scores from baseball games so I could analyze numbers and understand percentages. That emphasis seemed odd at first, but it all made sense when he subsequently taught me about different numbers on the business pages. Dad had been preparing me to study and analyze stock investments. I clearly remember the first time he took me to his stockbroker. Perhaps that's why I ended up marrying Angela, who, after she was a consultant on Wall Street, became a business school professor at Kansas State University and is now a financial broker. Yeehaw, Dad!

My old-school upbringing mirrored Booker T. Washington's conservatism, with its emphasis on education (a useful education, not studies in "ebonics") and a strong two-parent family with male and female role models to provide a proper social education, instill confidence, and encourage self-reliance.

These qualities provide the foundation for entrepreneurship, small business development, and prosperity. I remember "Sweet Auburn" Avenue and its vibrant black economy made up of businesses, law offices, and medical practices. We all aspired to be part of that. The Marine Corps HQ where Mom worked was located in the

Citizens Trust Bank building—a black-owned bank. We listened to WIGO and WAOK, two black-owned radio stations (and in case you were wondering, Mom was a high-pitched soprano whose warbling made my dad stick cotton balls in his ears). I grew up seeing successful black-owned businesses. Today my Cousin Naomi's husband, Bill Carroll, runs one of the biggest funeral homes in South Georgia, Jester's Funeral Home.

Through entrepreneurship you develop economic freedom, not economic dependency. Most important you develop a legacy to pass down through the family and across generations. Through economic freedom it is possible to break the bonds of disenfranchisement and gain greater influence, especially for the black community. The importance of entrepreneurship and economic freedom is what Washington understood more than a hundred years ago, and it's a legacy we must regain for our community today.

However, small businesses are being crushed under onerous regulations, higher and higher taxes, and limited access to capital. Self-reliance makes you politically important, but dependency makes you nothing but a pawn to be used in the chess match of political expediency. Auburn Avenue's vibrancy is lost, and its crumbling houses and boarded-up businesses reflect the condition of so many inner-city black communities.

The current black unemployment rate is double that of whites, and the black youth unemployment rate is much higher. How dire will these figures become when the market is flooded by millions of illegal immigrants with newly granted amnesty?

All Americans, black and white, see the results of black radicalism. The question is, for how much longer shall the black community follow the failed mantra of Du Bois? Where is the practical plan?

Booker T. Washington's black conservatism stood on the three strong pillars of education, self-reliance, and entrepreneurship. But I must add a fourth pillar, the one I believe is the strongest: Christian faith. The backbone of the black community is faith, the church. Heck, look at how most black leaders have titles of divinity. We all used to make jokes about the ol' Reverend Doctor, or "Rev Doc." Everywhere you turn there are Rev Docs.

Yet where was the black community when the 2012 Democratic National Convention held a vote to remove God from the party platform? Watch the video and hear how God was booed and rejected with a resounding no. Where was the outcry?

If W. E. B. Du Bois were to write *The Souls of Black Folk* today, how would he define our souls? Who are we, and what do we believe in? Du Bois called Washington's Atlanta speech a compromise, but it sure seems to me that by following Du Bois's ideology we compromised our principles and values. What legacy are we leaving for our next generation? And why should the black community support amnesty for illegal immigrants knowing the consequences for black unemployment?

There can be no doubt the soul of our soul is conservative. We were raised to see education, self-reliance, and entrepreneurship as the keys to economic freedom and liberty. Where did we take a wrong turn?

I suspect that by now, those of you with a different perspective are reading this and steaming. Good. Those of you who are black and who follow the progressive socialist ideology and philosophy are most likely shouting at these pages, calling me an Uncle Tom and a sellout.

In return, let me say *you* are the ones who are the Uncle Toms and sellouts. You have sold your own once regal and proud black community for less than thirty pieces of silver, and to what end?

Conservatism in black America is not new, but it's in dire need of a resurgence. Often I meet fellow blacks who pick me out of a crowd at the airport—my salt-and-pepper flattop is the giveaway—and too often they'll whisper to me that they like my message.

I have only one thing to say in response: Stop whispering.

The time has come to realize that *government* cannot restore our black community. The key ingredients of individual responsibility, industrialism, education, initiative, investment, and innovation, as well as the restoration of our culture and the family unit, must come from us, from our community. We must have leaders who will not sell us out for their personal political gain. The winds are changing. The time has come to bring back "old school" black values.

Booker T. Washington was right. The soul of our soul is conservative, not progressive—and certainly not socialist. It is only by hewing fast to conservative principles that we have any hope of ensuring a brighter future for our children and grandchildren and moving them off the twenty-first-century economic plantation.

Chapter 9

THE BIG LIE AND THE TWENTY-FIRST-CENTURY ECONOMIC PLANTATION

* * * * * * * * * * * *

At the bottom of education, at the bottom of politics, at the bottom of religion, there must be for our race, as for all races . . . economic independence.

—BOOKER T. WASHINGTON

It does not matter who is in power or what revolutionary forces take over the government: those who have not learned to do for themselves and have to depend solely on others never obtain any more rights and privileges in the end than they did in the beginning.

—CARTER G. WOODSON

A few months ago, I flew into Atlanta for a speaking engagement. I have to admit, my heart skips a little every time I go back home. I caught my first glimpse of the city during our approach for landing. Atlanta in springtime is a beautiful sight, full of lush trees and greenery. As the aircraft came in from the east, I could spy the downtown skyline from my aisle seat.

My destination on that day was in Cobb County. As I rode north up Interstate 85 toward downtown, my thoughts drifted back to the old days. We passed East Point, where my dentist practiced. We merged onto Interstate 75 and passed Turner Field (why didn't they name it Hank Aaron Field?). Right next door to Turner Field was the hospice where I last saw my mom. I will never forget the toughest day in my life, checking her in there with terminal liver cancer, knowing it was probably the last time I would see her alive.

We drove near where the old Fulton County Stadium once stood. I remembered taking the number six Georgia Avenue bus over there for baseball games, and how intimidating that arena was when it was packed for a Braves baseball game and Chief Noc-A-Homa got us going with the Braves chop. Used to cost about six dollars to get an upper-deck "nosebleed" seat . . . those were the days.

We went past the state capitol, with its dome gilded with gold mined from North Georgia, that remote part of the state where the US Army Ranger School conducts its grueling twenty-one-day Mountain Phase. Then we drove by my literal birthplace—little Hughes Spalding Hospital, dwarfed by the imposing Grady Memorial Hospital.

Then it hit me like a 105-millimeter artillery shell. As we passed the Edgewood Avenue exit off Interstate 75/85, I saw the empty shell of the community where I'd grown up. Auburn Avenue, once a haven for black entrepreneurs, doctors, and lawyers, now held only boarded-up and dilapidated buildings.

My ol' neighborhood, filled with fond memories, seemingly lost for the next generation. What had happened since the time of my birth in 1961? How had a vibrant community of churches, families, and prominent leaders faded away?

These are the questions I ask myself every time I go back to my hometown, and I'm quite certain many folks who grew up in inner-city neighborhoods puzzle over the same issues when they return home . . . if they return at all. I wonder what people feel when they go back and see Detroit? What emotions arise when former residents return to the South Side of Chicago?

I remember street ball and the corner basketball courts. Nowadays, most parents are too afraid to allow their kids outside to play for fear of gang violence and shootings. What bothers me is that many people who come from similar backgrounds and neighborhoods know exactly what I'm talking about, yet they remain silent. Well, we cannot be silent any longer.

When Buck and Snooks moved up to Atlanta, it was a different neighborhood. Yes, there was a struggle for equal opportunity, but as Booker T. Washington said, "Those who think there is no opportunity for them to live grandly, yea, heroically, no matter how lowly their calling, no matter how humble their surroundings, make a common but very serious error." My parents may have been on the lowest rung of the economic ladder, but they started a family—a unified black family—and made it strong and stable. They were surrounded by other black families. They went to church together. They possessed exceptional moral values that they passed down to us. Our role models weren't found on television or in stadiums; they lived right in our homes. Maybe we kids coveted the athletic prowess of Hank Aaron, but we wanted to emulate our moms and dads.

So what happened?

Why is it that the majority of the prison population is black? How is it that only 28 percent of our children live with both a mom and dad in their homes? How is it that we have surrendered the powerful moral values that made us the envy of other groups in America and now find ourselves drawn into a culture of moral depravity, drugs, and crime?

You want an example of depravity from my home state? Consider the death of thirteen-month-old Antonio Angel Santiago in Brunswick, Georgia. He was shot in the face in his baby stroller as his mother watched—and she was shot as well—during a failed robbery attempt. The perpetrators, ages seventeen and fourteen, were both black. How many of you have examples from your own community, in the neighborhood where you grew up? But the real question is, are you angry about it?

I don't mean feigned outrage directed at "Da Man." I mean anger at the people who promoted the big lie that government will solve your problems. Because I *am* angry about the mammoth, out-of-control social welfare entitlement programs from Washington, DC, that were supposed to solve our problems. The obvious truth is these impractical, politically motivated programs have irreparably damaged the fabric of our black society and community.

The irony is, we were told these policies would help us most of all, and yet our community has ended up being the most grievously harmed. To those who fell victim to the welfare mentality, I am sorry to say, you were sold a horrific lie. You are shackled to the twenty-first-century economic plantation. And just so you know, those of us who have escaped are not your enemy. We want nothing more than for you to be liberated as well, because you cannot continue to live in bondage.

The Republican Party was established for one reason:

the abolition of slavery through passage of the Thirteenth Amendment. Against the Democratic Party, the Republicans engaged in a fundamental philosophical fight for individual freedom from physical bondage. Today the fight for freedom continues with the same protagonists and antagonists, except now it is economic rather than physical bondage that must be defeated.

I find it especially ironic that Democratic president Franklin Delano Roosevelt said in his 1935 State of the Union address, "The lessons of history, confirmed by the evidence immediately before me, show conclusively that continued dependence upon relief induces spiritual and moral disintegration fundamentally to the national fiber. To dole out relief in this way is to administer a narcotic, a subtle destroyer of the human spirit. . . . The Federal Government must and shall quit this business of relief." But three decades later, another Democratic president, Lyndon Baines Johnson, did the exact opposite, administering the social narcotic of the Great Society programs.

There may have been some short-term merit to President Johnson's much-lauded Great Society and War on Poverty. But fifty years after these policies were enacted, all Americans must critically examine the residual effects. It troubles me greatly there exists such a sound bite mentality in America that we cannot ever dig beyond the superficial to determine the long-term effects of domestic and foreign policies. It appears that none of our elected officials take the time to analyze the unintended consequences of a particular policy decision, not only for the election cycle but for the next twenty, thirty, or forty years.

As I mentioned previously, President Jimmy Carter's Community Reinvestment Act of 1977 is a perfect example of shortsighted policy. The 2008 financial meltdown in the mortgage industry—a disaster even FDR could have foreseen—was directly related to Carter's policy of social engineering in the housing market under the guise of guaranteeing equality of achievement. Does anyone else get the feeling our current presidents don't study history when it comes to formulating policy?

In his book about President Johnson, *Big Daddy from the Pedernales,* author and historian Paul K. Conkin noted that Johnson's administration "moved beyond a response to pressing constituency pressures, beyond crisis-induced legislative action, to a studied, carefully calculated effort to identify problems and to create the needed constituencies to help solve them." Under Johnson the federal government greatly increased its intrusion into the economy and the lives of its citizens. According to Conkin, "In five years the American government approximately doubled its regulatory role and at least doubled the scope of transfer payments." There was a philosophic shift in the country from faith in the individual to a belief that government technocrats had all the answers.

During the Johnson years, faith in the government's

almost magical ability to solve problems reached a new high. Regardless of the issue, whether it was racial antipathy, unemployment, illiteracy, poor nutrition, inadequate housing, workplace accidents, insufficient cultivation of the arts, or environmental pollution, the response was simple: the federal government should do something or take a larger role in acting. In other words, the government needed to spend more money.

Conkin said, "Each of [the] Great Society commitments promised benefits to a targeted and often an increasingly self-conscious interest group (blacks, the aged, the educationally deprived, the poor, the unemployed, urban ghetto dwellers, consumers, nature enthusiasts)."

Consider one of the programs of the Great Society, the Food Stamp Act of 1964. Its original intent was to give low-income families access to nutritional foods grown primarily by American farmers. In 2013 the number of Americans on food stamps stood at nearly forty-seven million, up from thirty-two million when Obama took office. Heck, you don't need to use actual food stamps at the store anymore. Now the government sends money directly into an account that tops off the recipient's Electronic Benefits Transfer (EBT) card. Our government even spends taxpayer dollars to advertise enrollment for benefits—and not just for Americans. The USDA partners with the Mexican government to ensure migrant workers and Mexican nationals living in the United States are aware of the benefits.

Whiskey-Tango-Foxtrot?

Fifty years ago we waged a War on Poverty. Apparently we're getting our butts kicked, because from January 2009 to May 2013 we went from 39.8 million Americans in poverty to 49.1 million. The number of Americans on food stamps and living in poverty is greater than the entire population of Spain. Is this the legacy of the Great Society?

Sadly, I believe it is. I believe these programs were never meant to rectify problems but to increase dependency on government, all for political gain. Through the Great Society, the government created this economic plantation where the only real "benefits" are the electoral votes keeping the subsistence providers in power.

The government and its policies are destroying individual industriousness in order to promote individual subjugation and subservience. As a conservative, I believe in providing a safety net because I know there are those who are not as fortunate. But it shouldn't be a handout. It should be a hand up.

When I revisit my neighborhood in Atlanta, I see the blight facing most urban neighborhoods: Section 8 housing, food stamps, EBT card signs, and the breakdown of the family. Of all the consequences of the Great Society programs and the War on Poverty, intended or otherwise, the destruction of the black family has been the most disastrous. More than 70 percent of black children are born outside of marriage. That is an epidemic. And if you take into account the Centers for Disease Control and Prevention's statistics that close to three hundred thousand black babies are aborted annually, are we looking at racial genocide?

The brilliant idea for this tragedy came from the progressive socialists of the Johnson administration who thought government should provide welfare payments to women who purposely had children out of wedlock and did not seek to get married or have a male living in the same home.

In other words, the Johnson administration was promoting the disintegration of the moral fiber of the black community. Furthermore, the government would send out social workers to inspect the households and ensure there were no males residing in the home, because if there were, the benefits would be cut off. As long as women remained single, they could stay on these programs and receive free health care, housing, and babysitting services for life.

The most dangerous consequence of President Johnson's misguided policy is the abdication of individual responsibility in the black community. In 2010 the story of thirty-seven-year-old Angel Adams from Tampa, Florida, came to light. She has had fifteen children by three different men. Any sign of an adult male presence in her household? Of course not. Adams's famous quote should reverberate across America: "Someone's gonna pay for me and all my kids." Her story reflects the loss of individual responsibility not just among black women in urban areas but clearly among black men as well.

Now 60 percent of black children grow up in fatherless homes. There are some eight hundred thousand black men behind bars, and black men as a group have a one-in-three chance of serving time in prison at some point in their lives. And almost half of young black men in America's inner cities are neither working nor in school. As of April 2013, the reported black unemployment rate was nearing 14 percent; black teen unemployment was more than 30 percent. Black median family income is down, and approximately 32 percent of blacks live below the poverty line. Black businesses represent only 9 percent of start-ups in America.

This is social Armageddon.

Yet the so-called black leaders, nearly all of them Democrats, refuse to identify the true cause of these horrible statistics. And they give President Obama a pass. Even the former chairman of the Congressional Black Caucus, Emanuel Cleaver II, essentially admitted that African-American members of Congress hold Obama to a lower standard because the president is black. Regarding the disastrous level of African-American unemployment, Cleaver stated: "If we had a white president we'd be marching around the White House." Cleaver said, "The president knows we are going to act in deference to him in a way we wouldn't to someone white."

How is that not racist? Should not the same standard

be held for any leader? Has the black progressive leadership become so corrupt that it will sacrifice its own community for political gain?

And to think there are those who castigate Booker T. Washington as an Uncle Tom because he advocated self-reliance.

I find it reprehensible that some are willing to lead my people down the road to perdition rather than the road to success. If my own community never rises to the level of exceptionalism that other groups have been able to achieve, our nation will never achieve its full potential. America can never be any better or greater than the sum of its parts, and the black community is an integral part.

When Booker T. Washington talked about education, self-reliance, and entrepreneurship, he was describing economic independence. But the Great Society has left a legacy of economic *de*pendence, a new form of slavery, and to me, a far more dangerous one, because it destroys the will and determination to excel. As President Franklin Roosevelt said, welfare is "a subtle destroyer of the human spirit." And that is what I see when I go back to the ol' Fourth Ward and drive along Boulevard.

As historian Allen J. Matusow concluded, "The War on Poverty was destined to be one of the greatest failures of twentieth-century liberalism."

Since the mid-1960s, this nation has spent some sixteen trillion American taxpayer dollars on means-tested government income redistribution programs—in other words, welfare. Yet we have seen an increase in Americans on food stamps and in poverty, and the workforce participation rate is at its lowest since the Carter administration. The Great Society has turned out to be a big lie, and sadly, those in my community who bought into it are stuck on the twenty-first-century plantation.

Yet those of us in the black community who speak out are attacked. We are not just American ronin, but black ronin, lonely warriors who are shunned. Regardless, we remain the true guardians of our community and its conservative roots. We are the descendants of Booker T. Washington and will relentlessly defend his honor, vision, and belief in the self-reliance of our black community. We are proud and determined, and we shall not be silenced.

Chapter 10

THE HUNT FOR BLACK CONSERVATIVES

★ ★ ★ ★ ★ ★ ★ ★ ★ ★ ★ ★ ★

I always knew it would have to be a black president who was approved by the elites and the media, because anybody that they didn't agree with, they would take apart.

—Supreme Court Justice Clarence Thomas

On February 25, 2012, the headline read: "West: I'm Black by Birth Not by Choice" and it was front and center on a blog called Freewoodpost.com. The story covered an interview I supposedly gave John King on CNN. It featured quotes in which I appeared to reject my black identity and admit shame about who I was. It included a really oddball photo of me as well.

You can imagine the outrage and hate e-mails sent my way. Old friends still serving in the military called in disbelief. Even my own relatives picked up the phone to ask, "How could you?"

The only problem is, it never happened. There was never an interview with John King on CNN, and the so-called quotes had no quotation marks. But way, way, way at the end of the "story," there was a little disclaimer indicating that this website's content was purely satire. Now, how many people do you think noticed the disclaimer, let alone read it? And do you think either CNN or John King took the time to step forward and dispute the story or call out Freewoodpost.com?

Nah! Of course not.

The point of the Freewoodpost.com piece was to attack my character and, in the words of Justice Thomas, take me apart. I've lost count of the stories attacking my honorable service in the military and characterizing me as a war criminal—despite my honorable discharge. Because I like to ride a motorcycle and I occasionally wrote columns for an enthusiasts' magazine, I've been called a misogynist. It's frankly appalling. But if you read Saul Alinsky's *Rules for Radicals,* you'll see this is tactic number twelve: "Pick the target, freeze it, personalize it, and polarize it." Tactic twelve has been enthusiastically employed by the white liberal media and their black gatekeepers. The sad thing is, these shenanigans really seem to work—and what does that say about the general population?

I remember how in the film *The Hunt for Red Oc-*

tober, the US and Soviet Atlantic submarine fleets were seeking a state-of-the-art submarine. Now it's "the Hunt for Black Conservatives." We are relentlessly pursued by the entire fleet of liberal progressive media and elites. And their target is not limited to modern conservatives. For generations liberal historians have tried to destroy the legacy of Booker T. Washington. Why is it that any philosophy in the black community that differs from the established liberal canon is viciously attacked?

In 2013 a plainspoken yet astonishing man by the name of Benjamin Carson dared to break a taboo at the National Prayer Breakfast. In the presence of His Majesty President Barack Hussein Obama (and with cameras rolling), this brilliant pediatric neurosurgeon had the guts to challenge the dogma of the "community organizer" and question his brand of progressive socialism. Not surprisingly, after Dr. Carson's comments were broadcast across the nation, the hunt was on. Carson was immediately attacked and scrutinized for simply exercising his right to free speech.

However, what I find most disconcerting about this and other attacks on black conservatives is the manner in which the black community itself stands by and does nothing when white liberal progressives demean conservative blacks. In fact, some black folks even promote it.

During my reelection campaign in 2012, the opposition ran an advertisement depicting me with a gold tooth and boxing gloves punching white women, including a senior citizen, and stealing money from black families. Now, imagine if conservatives had run an advertisement like that against a black Democratic member of Congress? You wouldn't hear the end of it. In my case, however, there was no outcry from the usual suspects, such as Jesse Jackson, Al Sharpton, or Ben Jealous. As a matter of fact, when NAACP Senior Vice President for Advocacy and Washington Bureau Chief Hilary O. Shelton was asked about the advertisement in a TV interview, he replied, "I thought they made him look rather nice in a suit." Excuse me?

Deneen Borelli wrote about the overt practice of demonizing blacks who don't toe the progressive line in her book, *Blacklash*. She provides countless examples of the duplicitous hypocrisy of the Left, always crying racism against those who oppose their agenda and the twenty-first-century economic plantation.

In 1991, during his nomination hearings, the future Supreme Court justice Clarence Thomas took an unrelenting media beating that he described as "a high-tech lynching for uppity blacks who in any way deign to think for themselves, to do for themselves, to have different ideas, and it is a message that unless you kowtow to an old order, this is what will happen to you. You will be lynched, destroyed, caricatured by a committee of the US Senate rather than hung from a tree."

Today the hunt for the black conservative leads to a metaphorical tree, but the end goal is still death—career death. This relentless pursuit comes from the very same political party that gave the black community the Ku Klux Klan, Jim Crow laws, literacy tests, poll taxes, and literal lynching.

In 2004, during the search for weapons of mass destruction in Iraq, syndicated political cartoonist Jeff Danziger depicted then National Security Advisor Condoleezza Rice as a barefoot wet nurse. Danziger had Rice speaking like Prissy, Miss Scarlett's uneducated maid in *Gone With the Wind,* saying, "I knows all about aluminum tubes! (Correction) I don't know nuthin' about aluminum tubes." Where was the outcry from black leaders? Where were the protests and calls for Danziger to be fired and for all the papers running the cartoon to issue an apology?

All we heard at the time were crickets. Yet President Obama and the white liberal progressive media cried racism when UN Ambassador Susan Rice was challenged about her claims to the American people that the September 11, 2012, attack in Benghazi was simply a protest about a YouTube video that got out of hand.

There's nothing subtle about this, and there's no doubt the hunt is on. Just ask Harry Alford, Ken Blackwell, Deneen Borelli, Janice Rogers Brown, Herman Cain, Jennifer Carroll, Ben Carson, Ward Connerly, Larry Elder, Michel Faulkner, Niger Innis, Alphonso Jackson, E. W. Jackson, Kevin Jackson, Alan Keyes, Alveda King, Mia Love, Lenny McAllister, Angela McGlowan, Rod Paige,

Star Parker, Jesse Lee Peterson, Michael Powell, Tim Scott, K. Carl Smith, Thomas Sowell, Michael Steele, Shelby Steele, Lynn Swann, Tara Wall, J. C. Watts Jr., David Webb, Armstrong Williams, Walter Williams, Crystal Wright, and many others. They will tell you plainly that the attacks, the vitriol, and the disdain with which they must contend are unending. But we shall not be deterred from the fight.

The Left must destroy black conservatives because it cannot afford to have freethinking, independent-minded black Americans. If we begin to pull away from the dependency society and stand for the fundamental principles that once made us a proud community, the Left loses.

But when the Left wins, our community loses. The result of such blind loyalty is that many black voters have come to resemble Vladimir Lenin's "useful idiots." They make up an electorate that is completely taken for granted, and no one even bothers to listen. Why is it that a tiny special interest group can push gay marriage, but the black community stays mired in record unemployment? How is it that the Hispanic lobby can force an executive order on immigration policy, but the president relaxes the work requirement standards on Temporary Assistance for Needy Families (TANF), essentially keeping the dependency class growing? Why isn't there a strong voice addressing the issue of education in the black community? Why would there be, when one of

President Obama's first actions in 2009 was canceling the Washington, DC, school voucher program while sending his daughters to tony Sidwell Friends School?

Why don't the media address these issues?

Because as Justice Thomas said, the elites want someone who believes as they do—someone who supports progressive socialist policies. Nothing has changed since nearly two hundred years ago, when the Left supported W. E. B. Du Bois against Booker T. Washington.

The problem for leftists today is that they no longer face individuals who just fade away and stay in the shadows. When I travel across the country, I meet more and more blacks who come up and shake my hand in agreement. A new generation of young black conservatives is emerging. You find them hanging out with Andrew Simon and Richard Ivory at Hip Hop Republican. You see young bright lights springing up on college campuses—people like Nicholas Buford, a sophomore at Valdosta State University, and Langston Bowens, a freshman at Hillsdale College. I'm deeply encouraged by what I am seeing. Just as I believe there's a conservative resurgence in America in general, so shall it be in the black community.

The hunt for the black conservative is on, but slowly the hunter is becoming the hunted. In his superb documentary, *Fear of a Black Republican,* Kevin Williams delivers a spot-on analysis of a movement that is growing. There may not be a wholesale shift in the black community, but if we have enough movement, it will make a difference. The mainstream media have a clear tendency to recruit other blacks to denigrate and demean black conservatives. The mainstream media have sought to disrespect and deny the existence of black conservatism, but they're losing the battle—and they realize it. Heck, the fact that this book is being published is another counterstrike against the liberal progressive media. I fully expect it to be ignored or mercilessly picked at.

But as I've said, the soul of our souls is conservative. The big lie that has resulted in the twenty-first-century economic plantation will be exposed and defeated, and our community will be restored. Black conservatives are fighting back. Though our numbers may appear small, we have the tenacity of the three hundred Spartans. We are making a stand, and "we shall overcome, someday."

PART IV

THE FUTURE OF THE AMERICAN REPUBLIC

Chapter 11

REPUBLIC OR DEMOCRACY

✴ ✴ ✴ ✴ ✴ ✴ ✴ ✴ ✴ ✴ ✴ ✴ ✴

*The death of democracy is not likely to be an
assassination by ambush. It will be a slow
extinction from apathy, indifference and
undernourishment.*

— ROBERT M. HUTCHINS

*Dictators ride to and fro upon tigers which
they dare not dismount. And the tigers are
getting hungry.*

— SIR WINSTON CHURCHILL

When I'm in Washington, DC, my normal morning
routine is to get up early for a five- to six-mile run
from my "Batcave" down to the National Mall
and back. The symbols of our constitutional republic in
the early morning light are splendid to behold.

When I get back to my apartment, I flip on the local Christian radio station. Sometimes they're playing my favorite segment, the one in which schoolkids are reciting the Pledge of Allegiance—"and to the Republic for which it stands."

If there is to be a future for our nation, it means understanding America is a republic, not a democracy. The future of the American republic depends first and foremost on ensuring the citizenry and the voting electorate understand the basic framework of this grand experiment. When I'm speaking, I often pose this question: is America a republic or a democracy? Most people say it's the latter. How strange that schoolchildren can recite the Pledge of Allegiance yet don't understand what it means.

The failure of our education system to fully explain our republic isn't just an elementary, middle, or high school problem. On college campuses there are far too many political science departments following the dogma of Marx rather than Jefferson. Watch those "on the street" segments that Jesse Watters presents on Fox News, where average citizens are asked civics questions. It should send a chill down your spine when you realize how horribly disengaged the American electorate is. But if we were to hit the streets and ask about the latest episode of some reality show, it would be a different story.

As George Bernard Shaw mused, "Democracy substitutes election by the incompetent many for appointment by the corrupt few."

So just to set the record straight, I offer these contrasting definitions of a republic versus a democracy.

In its purest form, democracy is government of the masses, where authority comes from the direct expression of the crowd's will. In its worst expression, pure democracy can devolve into mobocracy, discontent, and anarchy.

The authority for a republic comes from public officials—I call them servants—elected by the people to represent their interests. In a republic the law is administered in accordance with established principles of justice. From its founding, America was designed to promote statesmanship, reason, liberty, justice, and advancement for its individual citizens. Lately, however, it seems some folks want to rebrand America as a representative democracy.

But that was never the intent of our Founding Fathers. In the Federalist Papers, Alexander Hamilton warned that "real liberty is never found in despotism or in the extremes of democracy," and John Adams had an even more dire prediction: "There never was a democracy yet that did not commit suicide."

That's why I have to laugh when people say we can bring "democracy" to other cultures and countries that don't understand the basic principles of individual liberty. It's not enough to "accept democracy" with the understanding that the majority rules and can impose its will, because groups that do not embrace the ideal of individual rights often see democracy as a way to kill off enough of the opposition to become the majority. Then these new regimes hold elections and say, "See, we have democracy, so we are a legitimate political entity."

Y'all don't believe me? Perhaps you've forgotten about Hamas in Gaza, Hezbollah in Lebanon, or the Muslim Brotherhood in Egypt?

My greatest fear is that if we don't pay attention, the loss of individual rights and the establishment of mob rule will happen here in America. In fact, I believe it's happening already. No one is literally killing the opposition, but character assassination is certainly executed frequently.

In the 2012 presidential election, Mitt Romney won approximately 75 to 78 percent of all the counties in America, but that didn't represent enough votes to win the election. Instead, because we've herded 51 percent of the population into urban centers representing under 25 percent of American counties, these few counties were enough to hand President Barack Hussein Obama a second term and, in his mind, a "mandate."

It may well be that from now on, all presidential election results will come down to a few counties in certain battleground states, while others—the "flyover states"—will be abandoned.

In that case we've come to a point where the president no longer needs to seek the support of a broad spectrum of the nation's citizens. Instead, to achieve victory, he needs to win over only a select group, centered around urban population centers.

Key voters' decisions and election results are no longer based on adherence to constitutional principles but instead on the promise of benefits made to a disengaged segment of the populace.

Critics may attack this assertion, but even Benjamin Franklin understood "when the people find that they can vote themselves money, that will herald the end of the republic." And James Madison warned that if government was not "derived from the great body of the society," it was in danger of being controlled by a "handful of tyrannical nobles."

So I ask you, when a presidential election hinges on a few urban centers, are we truly a representative republic? Regardless of the political party or the result, are we presenting meaningful arguments as to who can best govern the republic or are we simply bribing certain demographics in order to reach a magical number?

In 2013 I came across a fascinating essay titled "From Republic to Democracy; From Democracy to Kleptocracy; From Kleptocracy to Thugocracy," by former Marine officer Arthur L. McGinley, PhD. In the essay Dr. McGinley examines how the changes in several key policies began the shift from the original intent of the American republic.

Most noticeably he addresses the Seventeenth Amendment, which changed how we elected US senators. It was the founders' intent that senators be appointed by each state legislative body so they would be truly beholden to the state. But the Seventeenth Amendment made senatorial elections based on the will of the people. Dr. McGinley writes: "Rather than promoting legislation that strengthened the republic, all legislators now began to court the will of the uninformed masses."

I would say this is not just about the uniformed masses but also the un*informed* masses. I am reminded of the scene from *Gladiator* where young Emperor Commodus distracted the people of Rome from their real woes by giving them "panis et circenses," bread and circuses.

What do I see as the future for the American republic?

Well, Winston Churchill said it best: "Americans can be counted on to do the right thing . . . after they have exhausted all other possibilities." I believe the future of the American republic is actually strong and bright. I say this not as some blind ideologue but rather as an American statesman who knows his country.

We have indeed drifted away from our foundation as a republic, but in my travels, I am meeting more people of all ages who are asking about the Constitution. I see a rededication to who we are as a nation. Most encouragingly I see people challenging those who have been elected.

Yes, I lost a congressional election in 2012, but not once did I pander to voters and say what they wanted to hear. I told them what they *needed* to hear. Every day when I see my ugly mug in the mirror, I know I never surrendered my honor, integrity, or character for selfish political gain. Never did I target a certain demographic and offer them gold, and target another and offer them silver, and go before yet another and offer them bronze. Whether you agree or not, my message was always consistent.

As is written in Matthew 16:26, "For what is a man profited if he gains the whole world and forfeits his soul?"

The future of the American republic will be great if we find more men and women who put their country before personal or electoral gain. We will be exceptional as long as we demand the highest standards and accountability from those we elect.

But that means we must have the knowledge and guts to realize when we're being duped and to reject the politicized gimmicks. We'll know what's what in the next election cycle. I hope you and the rest of the electorate will be tuned in by then, because the republic for which we stand depends on it.

Chapter 12

THE DILEMMA FOR THE
AMERICAN REPUBLIC

☆ ☆ ☆ ☆ ☆ ☆ ☆ ☆ ☆ ☆ ☆ ☆ ☆

*Independence is the recognition . . . that
no substitute can do your thinking, as no
pinch-hitter can live your life.*

—AYN RAND

A s this book draws to a close, I want to capture some
thoughts I often share when speaking. The fate of
the American republic lies in the hands of her citizens. Our republic cannot survive if we continue to abdicate to others our freedom to choose.

And it's not just that we are abdicating the freedom, we're doing so without a clear understanding of the issues or the unintended consequences of our surrender. While the political scene in America has become deeply polarized along party lines, we've lost sight of how our decisions should be made: not based on party, but on principle—and an understanding of the issues.

Do I believe a third political party could arise in America? Yes.

However, it wouldn't be a party in the same vein as the Democrats and Republicans. It would be a party based on principles. Today the Democratic Party has drifted so far to the left it has lost touch with the fundamental values of our constitutional republic. The Democrats have truly embraced modern-day progressive socialism, and I would challenge anyone to show me where that model has ever been successful anywhere in the world. On the other hand, the Republican Party is slowly diluting itself into oblivion as it listens to talking heads saying it can only be successful as "Democrat Lite." Unsurprisingly, Democrat Lite has not proved to be a winning formula.

That leaves those of us who understand and support constitutional conservatism and the fundamentals of the American republic out in the cold. There are party establishments on both sides seeking to manipulate the political process to their liking. The so-called "mainstream media" are complicit in the deception of the American people—and consequently the people have ceased to trust them. (Fortunately the explosion of social media, blogs, and talk radio has made it harder to hide the corruption.)

The dilemma the American republic faces is this: shall we be an opportunity society or a dependency society?

As I write this chapter, America is faced with its highest rates of poverty, greatest number of food stamp recipients, largest number of people on Social Security disability, and lowest workforce participation rate. There can be no doubt we are moving away from creating opportunities for our citizens to making them dependent on government for their subsistence. In the past Americans have always chosen an opportunity society over a dependency society. But the social stigma of being dependent on government for subsistence has vanished—heck, these days it's almost fashionable.

How did we become a country where we advertise for people to sign up for welfare assistance, even if they live outside our borders? Do we really want to promote the expansion of the state at the expense of our own personal sovereignty and industrialism? Are we ready to give up those freedoms? Thomas Jefferson said it first: "A government big enough to give you everything you want is also big enough to take it away."

America's greatness was not built by an overarching centralized state but through the strength and resilience of its people. But bit by bit we are surrendering to politicians who stand not for our economic freedom but for economic dependence. The Left and its black gatekeepers went absolutely apoplectic some months ago when I used the word *enslavement*. But you tell me a better description for what social welfare dependence breeds. To me it's worse than physical enslavement, because it enslaves human spirit. It destroys the will and determination to seek improvement and a better life.

When it comes to fiscal, tax, regulatory, and monetary policy, we must choose between policies that will grow the private sector economy and those that will grow the public sector economy. While the stock market seems to be doing well for the moment, what would happen if the Federal Reserve stopped printing money? Furthermore, what does an exploding Dow Jones really mean for a struggling small business owner who cannot get a loan from his local small community bank because of the onerous regulatory mandates of Dodd-Frank?

When we choose between the opportunity society and the dependency society, we also choose between wealth redistribution (through an expanded government) and wealth creation. Progressive socialists think it's unfair that some have more than others and that in the name of economic fairness and social justice, we must force people to pay their fair share. But the reality is that we need policies that enable all to achieve prosperity and success. Constitutional conservatives believe in helping those less fortunate, but doing it by giving a hand up, not a handout. As I've mentioned before, we believe the safety net is there to catch those who may fall while climbing the American ladder of success. The net should help them bounce back up and continue to climb, not encourage them to lie there as if swinging in a hammock. Conservatives believe the best safety-net policy is simply to allow tax-exempt charitable contributions. As our "brothers' keepers," we can best determine how to help by assisting the local community, church, and charitable organizations of our choice. Instead we have the government in the business of expanding distress, despair, despondency, and destitution for its own political gain, and it becomes an insatiable consumer of individual and private sector capital to feed its social safety-net policies. The failure of Detroit and other inner cities demonstrates the ineptitude and inadequacy of central government welfare policies.

The opportunity society encourages exceptionalism. The dependency society encourages relativism and a necessary subjugation of the individual will to that of the state. The dependency society is about making everyone's success and ability relative to everyone else's. In the end the dependency society produces a graduating class of C students. The opportunity society produced two brothers who flew twenty feet in the air in 1903 and a man who flew to the moon and back just sixty-six years later.

The opportunity society tells individuals that their rights, as granted by their Creator, are life, liberty, and the pursuit of happiness. The dependency society confuses privileges with rights and sells *everything* as a right: the right to own a home, rights based on sexuality, a right to birth control—that one I can't really understand. What prevents manufactured women's rights advocate Sandra Fluke or anyone else from walking into CVS or Walgreens and picking up a pack of Trojans for the weekend?

When the state tells individuals everything is their right, eventually they will have no rights. It's a tactic employed by poll-driven hucksters to enable politicians to organize Americans into collective herds and drive them to their eventual slaughter. The herd mentality overtaking the American electorate will be its downfall. When we no longer see ourselves as individuals, we surrender the power granted by our Creator and fall for political gimmicks.

Such political gimmickry is part of the other dilemma confronting the American republic: the choice between politics and policy.

The republic cannot continue without policies promoting the fundamental governing principles established in our Constitution. We can't guarantee happiness, but we can promote policies that allow each of us to pursue happiness. Policy means telling people the truth and not pandering to collective groups. Unfortunately what we have now is politics full of insidious gimmicks.

For example, during the 2012 election cycle, we were bombarded with the idea of the 1 percent versus the 99 percent. We're all Americans, so aren't we all in the 100 percent? But Saul Alinsky's twelfth rule for radicals (isolate the target) works so well, why should the Left change tactics? And since the American electorate is so misinformed and so easily manipulated with the help of a complicit media, is it any wonder they fall for the Left's gimmicks? But America isn't about where you were born or where you're from. After all, how is it that thousands of refugees who arrived from war-torn Vietnam with literally nothing now have successful businesses and second-generation Ivy League–educated children? The whole 1 percent chant was just a political tactic with one aim: divide and conquer.

I'm sick of hearing politicians say, "I'm for the middle class, everything I do is for the middle class." I'm waiting for the leader who stands up and says, "I'm for America and all her citizens." There's no such thing as a fixed middle class in America. There's no caste system here preventing citizens from rising to whatever level of achievement they desire.

But through political gamesmanship, barriers to success are created, with the only solution being government-driven guarantees of achievement, outcomes, and results. Then social engineering usurps individual will and replaces it with the statist goal of turning people into "sheeple."

Politics gave us the abject insanity of the "War on Women" in the 2012 election cycle. I will never forget Sandra Fluke taking the stage at the Democratic National Convention in Charlotte, North Carolina, to talk about women's rights, followed by that celebrated serial adulterer, former president Bill Clinton. Hypocrisy, anyone?

That's the nature of politics. Through microtargeting and divisive segmentation, the political machine figures out what buttons to push to maintain power. And voters fall for it over and over again. They reward the impostors and charlatans.

This dilemma, between politics and policy, is what Americans must overcome to safeguard the future of our republic. Do we want to elect statesmen or pop culture icons? Do we now believe all it takes to lead is to be fun and cool? Statesmen recognize the issues and provide solutions—not sound bites, but principle-based results that will benefit the safety and security of this nation. I fear national-level elections have become nothing more than a version of *American Idol.*

It always makes me laugh when someone comes up to me and says, "You're Allen West, right? Well, I don't agree with anything you stand for." When I ask them, "Exactly what is it you disagree with?" they're always unprepared, and their response is always, "Well, I don't want to get into that here." I love being able to respond, "C'mon, what is it, you don't think we need tax reform to promote small business economic growth? You don't think we need to develop our own energy resources in order to stop sending taxpayer dollars to those who want to kill us? Don't you believe in getting away from occupation-style warfare to more strike-oriented operations?" And on and on, as they stand bewildered.

Too many Americans are no longer paying attention, and so they too stand bewildered. Yet we must all answer the question ourselves or have it answered for us: what do we want for the future of our American republic?

Do we want an opportunity society, or a dependency society?

Do we prioritize preeminence of the individual, or dominance of the state?

Will we choose individual exceptionalism, or collective relativism?

Do we value wealth creation and expansion, or wealth redistribution?

Will we bet on economic freedom, or economic enslavement?

Do we stand for principle, or for party?

Do we want policy, or politics?

After you answer for yourself, think about the legacy you'll leave your children and grandchildren. Will it be a legacy of liberty, or servitude?

I am constantly amazed that standing strong for liberty has made me an outcast, an American ronin, to so many. But I cannot believe I'm the only one who will step forward to be a guardian of this American republic. At least I hope I'm not.

Chapter 13

SERVANT LEADERSHIP VERSUS SELF-SERVICE

☆ ☆ ☆ ☆ ☆ ☆ ☆ ☆ ☆ ☆ ☆

> *If ever a time should come, when vain and*
> *aspiring men shall possess the highest seats*
> *in Government, our country will stand in*
> *need of its experienced patriots to prevent*
> *its ruin.*
>
> —SAMUEL ADAMS

If there is to be a long and healthy future for our republic, there must be a restoration of servant leadership. At the time of this writing, our nation is embroiled in countless political scandals.

In Benghazi, on the eleventh anniversary of 9/11, our embassy in Libya came under attack. The greatest and most powerful nation in the world did nothing. Two former US Navy SEALs fought to defend sovereign American soil against Islamic terrorists, and they too were abandoned. They were ultimately killed, along with the ambassador and one other American. Many more were seriously injured. Afterward, members of the Obama administration purposefully altered intelligence reports and misled the American people. Yet administration spokespeople and pundits say this is irrelevant, a joke, and a circus sideshow.

The Internal Revenue Service has been caught targeting certain Americans and groups based upon political ideology and other beliefs that happen to be contrary to those of the party in power. Tax records have been leaked. Nonprofit applications delayed. Yet once again we hear "there is no there, there" and this is all just a deception. Some progressive socialist pundits, such as Lawrence O'Donnell at MSNBC, even agree that Americans should be targeted and that the IRS acted appropriately. "Revered" individuals like Julian Bond, president emeritus of the NAACP, compare the constitutional conservative grassroots movement, the Tea Party, to the Taliban. We have an attorney general who manipulates the truth and has targeted members of the free press.

And yet there are no consequences, no ramifications, and no condemnations.

How did we come to this point? How is it that the arrogance of officialdom has become so blatant that someone like Lois Lerner of the IRS can plead the Fifth and be sent away on "paid leave" at a cost of $177,000 to American taxpayers?

We have become so enamored with the cult of personality in America that we wouldn't recognize a servant leader if he or she walked up and shook our hand. We have accepted tyrannical demagoguery as the norm. Even worse, in the case of President Barack Hussein Obama, we have lowered the standard of leadership to having a nice smile, giving a good speech (with teleprompter), and being likable.

I believe the election and reelection of Obama were among the most conspicuous acts of denial in recent years. Voters just stopped paying attention. They accepted consistently bad behavior and rewarded it. Then they wonder why they get more bad behavior. Of course many in opposition dare not challenge the behavior because they're too obsessed with race and political correctness.

In Obama's case we've enabled affirmative action to find a home in the nation's highest office. There you have it. I said it and I stand by it. America fell for the gimmick candidate, disregarding every fact and warning sign in the rush to have "the first African-American president." We were told to shut up, and a complicit media became part of the scheme.

What's next? What type of gimmick will we rush to accept as a leader regardless of qualification, leadership, or principles? The first Hispanic president? The first gay president? The first transgender president? The first

Muslim president? (Oh, wait . . .) How long will we follow destructive cults of personality just to appease the gods of political correctness?

If there is to be a future for this republic, we must elect good leaders, not highly marketed, well-politicized petty usurpers and impostors. The nation has become so infatuated with the politics of personal attacks and character assassination that we sit back and allow political ads to drive our decision-making process.

Will we ever reclaim the sense of character found in those early patriots who gave us the great blessing of liberty?

We're not being governed, we're being ruled by incompetence. But everyone is still having fun, right? At least our president is. He hobnobs with pop stars and celebrities and plays lots of golf. His wife has nice clothes and a new hairstyle and gets lots of magazine covers.

You see, sometimes we get the government we want, but this time we got the government we deserve. We deserve this because we've stopped believing in holding elected officials to a higher standard. We deserve this because we're too lazy to do due diligence and recognize when we're being deceived. We deserve this because we reject the truth in order to accept the lie that makes us feel good. We have become comfortable with living selfishly in the now rather than ensuring a lasting legacy.

We've become a joke.

Why has our nation become lost? Lack of honor, integrity, and character in our elected officials is a bipartisan issue that has infected both sides. When did we start living in Bizarro World where up is down, right is wrong, everything is inverted, and nothing is as regular order would have it be?

It happened the day we started to devalue true leadership. Our nation's leaders no longer seem to have a moral compass. Unlike the samurai—or even the ronin—they have no code of honor.

One of my top five favorite movies is *The Last Samurai*. While not historically accurate, the film portrays the late-nineteenth-century shift in Japanese culture and that country's Westernization. Of course my favorite character was Lord Katsumoto, who embodies the essence of the samurai, one who serves. Katsumoto, along with all samurai, devoted his life to seven moral principles, the code of Bushido, which is the way of the warrior:

Rectitude (gi)—Principles of moral virtue

Courage (yu)—The ability to face difficulty, danger, or pain fearlessly

Benevolence (jin)—The desire to help others and prevent selfish arrogance

Respect (rei)—Esteem for excellence (Of course, I learned in the US Army that respect is earned, not given.)

Honesty (makoto)—Fairness and the attempt to do your best at all times

Honor (meiyo)—Integrity in your beliefs and actions

Loyalty (chugi)—For me that means loyalty to my
family and the core principles of God and
country

I loved that movie because of Lord Katsumoto's selfless devotion to the principles of his code. I too am inspired by a code, to be all I can be and to always seek to improve. That is my code of Bushido.

I chose the title *American ronin* because I have been characterized as something of an outcast. There are those who try to dishonor me and my service to this republic. But I will forever pledge my sword to the defense of this great nation—not for myself, but for my country and for the legacy I can secure for my children. I have lived an imperfect life, but I have sought perfection in my service to this nation.

We need men and women who embody a code of service not to themselves but to this republic and its core principles. We need a citizenry that will not settle for the lesser of two or three evils but that will recognize and demand truly principled and selfless leadership.

We do not need more "political family royalty" in America, nor individuals who believe they are entitled to office. We need term limits in our federal elected offices, including the House of Representatives and the Senate. No one should stay a member of the House or Senate longer than twelve years. I believe the more time people spend in Washington, DC, the further removed they get from the people who sent them there. As Thomas Jefferson said, "Whenever a man has cast a longing eye on offices, a rottenness begins in his conduct."

I know the future of this American republic is secure because we always seem to find a new generation of principled leaders at just the right time. We know something is amiss in America, and there are many who fear for the future. But I say fear not! Sometimes we have to hit rock bottom to learn the important lessons.

Ronald Reagan's 1964 speech "A Time for Choosing" is often quoted, and there's a reason why. He perfectly captured the uniqueness of this nation and how tenuous is our hold on what makes it so. Even now, a half century later, his words are relevant:

> *If we lose freedom here, there's no place to escape to. This is the last stand on earth. And this idea that government is beholden to the people, that it has no other source of power except the sovereign people, is still the newest and the most unique idea in all the long history of man's relation to man.*

It is indeed our time to choose.

PART V

CONCLUSION

Chapter 14

BRAVO-FOXTROT-OSCAR

✶ ✶ ✶ ✶ ✶ ✶ ✶ ✶ ✶ ✶ ✶

*I belong to the warrior in whom the old ways
have joined the new.*

—Lord Katsumoto in *The Last Samurai*

In the military we truly love acronyms—some folks
even get achievement medals just for coming up with
new ones. Some of the acronyms that will never get an
award are MRE—Meals Rejected by Everyone; CRS—
Can't Remember "Stuff" (we actually use a different
word for stuff, but this is after all a G-rated book);
FUBAR—"Messed" Up Beyond All Recognition (ditto);
and MSH—Make "Stuff" Happen (ditto again).

BFO stands for a Blinding Flash of the Obvious—
which is what I intended you to take away from this
book. Through my life story and my commitment to this
country, I want to challenge Americans to think about

what our nation was, what it is now, and what it shall be. I believe the answers are right before our eyes. We just have to take the time to make an informed choice.

We have to turn off the brain-draining reality TV shows for a few hours and read, think, assess, and challenge ourselves to be better.

My last duty assignment in the US Army was at Fort Hood, Texas, in the Fourth Infantry Division. The division has a long-standing and heroic history of service in combat to our nation, and I was honored to serve in the "4ID" in combat as a battalion commander in Iraq. The division's motto comes from its theme song:

Steadfast and loyal, we're fit to fight,
The nation's finest soldiers keep liberty's light,
Our soldiers roar for freedom,
We're fit for any test,
The mighty 4th Division, America's best.

So, as with all correspondence I write, I will sign off and conclude this, my first-ever literary project, with those three simple words:

Steadfast and Loyal.

ACKNOWLEDGMENTS

I want to thank God for giving me the courage to stand on principle and blessing me in countless ways.

I want to thank my wife of twenty-four years, Angela Graham-West, PhD, who has always been there through good times and bad and who has pushed me beyond my perceived limits to excel. I thought that earning two master's degrees would put me in the same intellectual league with her, but no such luck.

I want to thank my darling daughters, Aubrey Elizabeth (call sign Chili Bean) and Austen Brianna (call sign Beetlejuice) for understanding my commitment to our country and their future and why Dad has often been away. They've truly been troopers and have always given me the best hugs. And thanks to Wangying Lin (call sign Linny Lin), who came into our lives as an exchange student from China and quickly became a loving member of our family.

I want to thank sister-in-law Joann Williams-West for her spiritual support and for providing the keepsake pictures. And to my nephew, Major Herman Bernard West II, the fourth man in the West family to serve the republic. I'm so proud of you, young man. Doggone, I used to bounce you on my knee, and now you are just one promotion away. . . .

I want to thank Michele Hickford, my cowriter, who took my words and edited them into this finished product. It's tough editing for a Southerner—we still have that subject-verb agreement issue. As well, Michele is my dive buddy, and after all this she's probably planning a real nice live-aboard dive trip somewhere. Michele, you are the consummate professional, and I am so thankful for the day we met onboard the South Florida Diving Headquarters catamaran four years ago.

I want to thank Dana Perino, who dialed me up and simply said, "You need to write a book." She may be tiny in stature, but she certainly makes it up in her resolve. Dana, thanks so much for believing this was something I could accomplish.

And thanks too to the impeccable team at Penguin Random House: Rick Horgan, Campbell Wharton, and Nathan Roberson—and Sean Desmond, with whom I started. What an incredible honor that a young fella from the inner city of Atlanta could grow up and be published by one of the most recognized publishing houses in the world. I cannot thank you all enough for taking my raw thoughts and converting them into this final work. This is something I shall never forget, and it will be part of the legacy I leave to Chili Bean and Beetlejuice.

And to all my friends and fellow patriots—as well as my

detractors and critics—I hope you'll enjoy this book. Don't know if I will do this again, but it sure was fun this time.

Mom and Dad, thanks for raising me to be the disciplined man I am. May you smile just a little brighter up there in heaven knowing your legacy lives on.

INDEX

Index